BECAUSE THERE WAS
Margoth
ONE GOOD DEED SERVES ANOTHER

INSPIRED BY TRUE EVENTS
Jeffrey Hartman

—— MVHL ——

Copyright © 2022 by Jeffrey Hartman

Because There Was **MARGOTH** One Good Deed Serves Another

All rights reserved. No part of this publication may be reproduced, distributed, or transmitted in any form or by any means, including photocopying, recording, or other electronic or mechanical methods, without the prior written permission of the publisher, except in the case of brief quotations embodied in critical reviews and certain other noncommercial uses permitted by copyright law. For permission requests, write to the publisher, addressed "Attention: Permissions Coordinator," at info@labricollective.com

Quantity sales special discounts are available on quantity purchases by corporations, associations, and others. For details, contact the publisher at info@labricollective.com

Orders by U.S. trade bookstores and wholesalers.
Email: info@labricollective.com

Creative contribution by Jennifer Plaza
Cover Design - Low & Joe Creative, Brea, CA 92821
Illustrations - Len Westerberg
Book Layout - DBree, StoneBear Design

Manufactured and printed in the United States of America distributed globally by markvictorhansenlibrary.com

MVHL

New York | Los Angeles | London | Sydney

ISBN: 979-8-88581-003-6 Hardcover
ISBN: 979-8-88581-004-3 Paperback
ISBN: 979-8-88581-005-0 eBook

Library of Congress Control Number: 2022904716

DEDICATION

There are people in the world that have such a profound influence on your life that you strive to become a better person because of them. I have been blessed to have two such people in my life. The first is my extraordinary wife of over forty years, Katherine, who is the biggest supporter of the work I do, and encouraged me to write this book. Kathy has travelled with me to serve internationally on many occasions, and the benefit I receive from her unique perspective on the needs of the women we serve is priceless. Kathy is responsible for the fact that our organization focuses almost exclusively on helping women, having persuaded me that empowering women will change their communities and the world. This book is dedicated to you, Kath. You make my life worth living.

With Gratitude

I also owe an extreme debt of gratitude to my dear friend, the late Dr. Timothy Wall, MD. Tim was the founder of the CareLink Foundation, the organization that I now lead and under which we do our micro-finance work. Tim was at my side when we presented the real "Margoth", the inspiration for this book, with her initial micro-finance loan many years ago. Tim was taken from us suddenly in 2018, was a faithful and tireless servant of God, and his compassion and love for those in need is legendary. Tim taught me the meaning of "Love your neighbor."

Jeffrey Hartman
Naperville, Illinois

PROLOGUE

There are moments in our lives when a witnessed good deed monopolizes the mind of the observer. The remnant ravelings of that act and the following butterfly effect leaves them in awe. When something so small as a bit of cash and words of encouragement empower a single woman to embrace her dreams and share her gifts, a miracle occurs. The business prowess emerges, and the fortune becomes that of the surrounding community.

People within that community may include those in institutions such as shelters, hospital wards, or orphanages. These realities pull at the observer's heart which begs for a way to cease the cruelty. Ideas ensue, the butterfly takes flight, and the goodness is spread. The chain reaction born from circumstance and observation.

This is the story of a woman, much like my dear friend, who stood strong and took a leap of faith in her own gifts and dreams. Her determination and focus on making her business thrive led to her service to underprivileged women, inspiring them to help others even more less fortunate than they. This story is a tribute to my wonderful friend Margoth, and the power of the adage, "One good deed, serves another."

CONTENTS

Prologue		6
Chapter 1	2001 Post Hurricane Mitch	11
Chapter 2	Feliz Cumpleaños	19
Chapter 3	New Friends	31
Chapter 4	Inspiration	39
Chapter 5	2002 Opening Day	51
Chapter 6	Spring 2002	61
Chapter 7	Injustice	71
Chapter 8	Resistance	79
Chapter 9	2006 Overcoming	89
Chapter 10	Finding Peace	103
Chapter 11	2011 Small Gifts	117
Chapter 12	2021 Hope	127
Epilogue		134
A Readers' Guide		147
About the Author		164

Chapter 1
2001
POST HURRICANE MITCH

12 | Jeffrey Hartman

2001 Post Hurricane Mitch

"Carmen!" the tanned face commanded. It belonged to a twenty something woman with flowing black hair. Not flowing in the sense of Hollywood style and flare, but with an untamed windswept mass of black strands that covered her face and caught on her lashes. The sun gleamed overhead and reflected a sort of maroon hue or highlight from those defiant locks. Her face was taut, a grimace that reached her eyes. The kind of look that says, "I've had enough." And in her failed attempt to smooth the disparaging strands and stay out of the road from the jeep that roared past with the gunmen glaring at all who dared occupy the streets, she gathered her skirt in one hand. With the other she tucked a younger version of her likeness behind her. "You stay behind me."

Gun shots echoed in the emptying Honduran streets. The driver fired into the air. A reminder that the people did not matter, but that may not be true. For argument's sake, I dare say they needed the people. The people who gave them the rise through fear. Without fear there would be no compliance. They needed compliance to push their agenda. In the end people are the root to all that is. Perhaps they knew and it was this woman who discovered their cognitive prowess. Either way, it is fact. These street thugs needed people to fear them.

Another burst of gunfire.

The young girl hid behind her brazened human shield. The litany of bullets permeated the air. The smell of diesel exhaust and gunpowder now engulfed the hard-faced woman. She locked eyes with one particular gunman as he drove by. He smiled at her. The woman stayed expressionless. No cowering, no antagonizing with a cocked brow, and no spoken words. The men drove off from the town square continuing their gunfire and terrorism.

"Margoth, he could have killed you," the younger girl said. Where her older counterpart maintained a callous visage, the girl exhibited the opposite. She had wet lashes and tear streaks through the thin layer of dirt that settled on her olive sun-kissed skin. "What good would your death do me, or mama? Anyone?"

"My death would buy time for your escape, Carmen. I'd rather die protecting my little sister than have those men think they can take what they want. Must I remind you that if I died you would have a chance. They could have just taken us, but they don't want stubborn and ugly." Margoth took the edge of her gathered skirt and blotted her sister's eyes. "If God wills it, I will find a way to get our town back, hermanita. I promise." She put her arm around the young girl, who was to celebrate her sixteenth birthday that evening, and ducked into an alley.

The jeep roared in the distance, their gunfire now a series of pops. Halted cars took to the roadway and a woman in a brilliant orange, blue, and yellow skirt bustled from the roadside. The street carts with baskets filled with mangos, coconuts, and other local produce shunned her offering, a mere two cents short. The vendors followed her receding figure. Even they could not hope to make six dollars today.

#

Since the Banana Republic days of the early 20th Century, Honduras has suffered decades of governmental corruption, coups, military conflict, and international meddling. The result is a country suffering from extreme poverty and social injustice. One third of the population lives on less than one dollar per day. Women and children, as is often the case, suffer the worst. Honduran women, victims of severe sexual and economic discrimination, are only half as likely as men to be employed. Making matters much worse, Honduran religious norms frown upon birth control. This reality, coupled with an aggressive "Machismo" male mind-set embedded in the culture, causes untold unwanted pregnancies—more mouths that women can not feed.

Honduras is one of the poorest countries in the Western Hemisphere, and those born there are said to have lost the "geography lottery." This is even more tragic when considering the country's beauty, potential, and lovely people. Local organizations, NGOs, and missionary groups work diligently to address poverty and injustice are often overwhelmed by governmental corruption and stolen resources. Gangs and poverty-driven crime further contribute to the difficulties endured by the people of Honduras, many of whom are good and hard-working people just trying to stay alive.

Extreme poverty means half of Honduran children do not attend school, either because their parents can not afford school supplies, or the children's services are needed to help the family earn a meager living.

Well intended Christians on short-term mission trips flood Honduras by the plane loads, providing much-needed money, temporary medical clinics, and food. Those groups, however, typically stay for a week or so, and then head back to the comforts of their North American homes, and things in Honduras remain largely unchanged. The cycle of misery and desperate poverty are re-born as soon as the visitors leave. While the spiritual encouragement of these groups is helpful and welcome, their efforts—with the exception of sharing the Gospel, of course—do little to address the root cause of the suffering.

Hurricane Mitch ravished Central America in 1998. More than 7,000 Hondurans lost their lives. The country was left devastated, crops and infrastructure were destroyed from winds that reached 189 mph, flooding, and mudslides. Rebuilding happened for those with the capital to do so. Missionaries piled on planes to help local women and children left penniless. They brought water, food, medical supplies, and money, though the money in the hands of many of the men went for alcohol and various drugs. The women used it to buy food for their children and neighbors. With the fields void of legumes and fruits, there were few jobs and provisions. The country was in a constant state of recovery.

This morning the sun baked the asphalt roads in the Central American heat. VW vans chugged along revving and stopping from random dogs and running children. Dust kicked up behind a rusted bus that wove between women carrying screaming babes and calloused barefoot girls. The smell of exhaust permeated the yellow dust. The bus driver honked, the horn a weak whine. The rack atop was overfilled with bags, a crated chicken, and a wooden chair that seemed too common back in the States. Three or four people, often an entire family, can often be seen speeding through town on a motor scooter, in a country in which a car is often an unthinkable luxury. A dark-haired American stood aloof from the chaos, his fresh denim jeans and white cotton polo drew staring eyes.

"How we take for granted that little piece of comfort, nay—luxury," he whispered.

Nueva Suyapa, Honduras in 2001 was alive with merchants, women, children, missionaries, and gangs. The government was in upheaval leaving its citizens to fight for food, education, and justice. Rifles and bullet filled belts swaddled men whose determined faces taught the women and children it was better not to be seen and never heard. That is, until Margoth.

Chapter 2
FELIZ CUMPLEAÑOS

Feliz Cumpleaños

Carmen burst through the whitewashed pine door, "Mama, mama." She dropped her basket with fresh mangos by the wall and hugged the middle-aged woman.

Carmen and Margoth's mother, Rosa Cruz, was in her prime at thirty-eight, with black hair braided in a line that extended to her hips. She was a petite woman, a mere 4 feet 11 inches and wore hand sewn moccasins hidden by a bright blue skirt. In the afternoon hours, when the sun was at its peak, she worked indoors. On a normal day she mixed masa with water to make papusas with queso if they had it. Papusas were a staple in the Cruz home, but today was different. It was Carmen's birthday.

Rosa stood by a large Pine board table, defeathering a chicken for Carmen's special day. She planned to make tamales, her daughter's favorite. The fresh chicken would go into the pot with the red beans she had soaking in a large clay bowl by the kitchen window. The kitchen was a small area with a wood fire stove and no refrigerator. There was no indoor plumbing and no sink. Instead, she used water kept outside in a cistern. There was an old yellow painted dresser by the turquoise wall that Rosa kept the dinner plates and cutlery in. Since there was no counter, the table served as the butcher block, washing station, and dining place.

The house had been a labor-rich abode made of concrete blocks and a tin roof that needed constant repairs. It was Margoth's childhood home. In the middle of the one room house was a fireplace. The terracotta tiles alternated between blue and white glaze with rough natural pieces. Flames danced in the pit illuminating the hand painted designs. The bright colors stood out in the pale white room. They seemed to come alive with each lick of reflected flame. As a child she would trace the intricate flower patterns and diamond cuts with her fingers.

When her mother was fourteen, Margoth was born. She told Margoth how she had given birth to her in front of that fireplace. In the woes of pain, Rosa watched the dancing flames to keep herself grounded. She told Margoth that tracing the lines on the tiles made her realize that hard work and focus would get her through the toughest times. Though she wasn't alone; her mother and the local women helped her through the birth. And Margoth's father was nowhere to be found. According to Rosa, it was a good day when he left and never came back, as so many Honduran men have done. She had her beautiful Margoth, and God to guide her.

As Margoth grew, she also learned the cool smooth glaze's secrets. The bumps from the artisan's fingertips mesmerized her.

She was much like her mother, and proud. They loved intricate patterns enlivened with bright colors. But they also recognized hard work and determination.

#

Carmen came along nine years later. She was born in that same house, with Margoth and a midwife by her mother's side. Margoth's grandmother had died of influenza just a year prior. Carmen's father was a farmhand. He was gunned down four months into Rosa's pregnancy. Since it was the three of them, Margoth cared for Carmen while Rosa worked piecemeal jobs to keep food in their bellies and the home she created. Now that Carmen was old enough, the three women worked wherever they were needed. School was not an option after fourteen.

#

"You girls must be hungry," Rosa said as she smiled and tilted her head for her daughters to kiss her cheek. "Tortillas are there, have some salt. I have a special dinner for my special girl."

Carmen grabbed a tortilla from the terracotta plate. Margoth stood in the doorway. She pulled the worn blue linen curtains aside to allow the sun's light to liven the cool space. It was a small solid house. "Need help, mama?"

"Fetch me some water and rinse the rice, m'hija. This chicken needs a good rinse, then…"

"Then the ladies will be at the door waiting for a taste of your tamales!" Margoth, teased.

Rosa smiled and kissed Margoth's cheek as she used her apron to wipe the table. Carmen carried the canvas bag of masa flour to the table nibbled her tortilla. Margoth grabbed a metal bowl to mix the dough.

#

In their small-town outside the capital city of Tegucigalpa, the Honduran community of women were strong. Margoth knew that the neighbor ladies would come to celebrate her sister's birthday, but more than that, they would come for the food. She went door to door asking for a small bit of beans, masa and rice from the women she knew could spare a bit. The chicken came from a merchant in town they bought weeks before. Although they hadn't planned to eat it. They used it for eggs until it got caught by a wild dog and had to beat it off the day before.

#

Margoth heard Carmen yelling, "Get off!" She ran outside to see Carmen kick the skinny wild dog. It dropped the chicken but grabbed their second and ran off. Margoth grabbed the ax from inside their doorway and gathered the injured chicken into her arms. She said a quick prayer and chopped of the head to put it out of its misery. Even though they would eat well with it, the three worried, with both their chickens gone the egg supply was depleted. They had to save to get another.

#

Rosa had prepared the banana leaves for the tamales the day before.

Carmen and Margoth had made a piñata to hang in the yard. Rosa had a good quarter pound of red beans, a full pound of masa, and maybe half of rice. It was a good amount of food. Enough to feed themselves and the expected company of maybe six women and eleven children, providing their husbands let them.

Margoth helped most with the tamales, a traditional Honduran dish. It took love and care. First, she had to prepare the white masa which had ground corn, green chiles, onions, and salt. Next, she prepared the red masa. That was her favorite. She liked the smell of chicken cooking with achiote, garlic, onions, and sweet chiles. The meat would be mixed into a separate ground corn base to make the dough. It was a labor of love. Though the chiles were dried and the onion small, it was a feast.

#

The sun would disappear on the horizon in two hours. Margoth lit the firepit Carmen constructed for cooking meals, after the hurricane came through. It was a hole in the ground with stones lining the edges. It was good for cooking potted dishes like beans and rice with coconut milk.

Carmen stepped up to her sister, "We should have just run. You could have died on my birthday."

Margoth embraced her sister and took her hands. "Carmen, there is no right way with those men. I am too old now. They will not look at me the same ways as you." She kissed her sister's cheek. "Now, it's time."

Four women walked in haste to the small yard. Each had their children close to their heels. One woman in a blue pair of slacks with a bright pink blouse was accompanied by the gentleman observer Margoth noticed in town. There were twenty tamales and seventeen people. She had not accounted for the stranger, which meant she would give him her dinner had the missing three women shown. She also knew that if her sister saw her without, she would offer her own, and that in the end, Rosa would insist that they both eat, and go without for herself.

One neighbor woman dressed in a worn white dress hugged Margoth, "For one night, there would be full bellies for us all." She glanced back at her three small children.

Margoth smiled the kind of smile that said she understood. The woman, señora Ramon, had five children. Two died shortly after birth from malnutrition. She often gave her food to the little ones left. They, like nearly half of the children in rural Honduras, showed signs of poor nutrition; lethargy, poor concentration, and a sickly demeanor, and all were still under ten. It is well known that these silently-suffering children will face a lifetime of the effects of a chronically poor diet; stunted development, learning disabilities, and illness. It was a common scene but one that still brought tears to Margoth's eyes. It was known that starvation led to fatty liver which had the tendency to develop into cirrhosis and eventually death if it persisted.

The observer was clean shaven and had denim jeans and a white polo shirt. All the women knew he was a missionary, but one they had not seen before. He smiled at the children as they ran past him.

"Good evening. My name is George Jacobs, and I was invited by the pastor to meet you. I am from MercyLink, a service organization from the United States."

"Welcome," Rosa said and kissed his cheek. "Would you do the honor of saying grace?"

"I would be honored." The young man, cleared his throat, drawing attention from all the children and their mothers. A hush encompassed the small group as George began to pray, "Dear Heavenly Father, as we thank you for the food we are about to receive, I ask that you bless these women and their children. Today is Carmen's sixteenth birthday and we have gathered together to honor her this day. We see the wonders you bestow upon us and receive your gifts with grace. I also want to thank you, for bringing me to Nueva Suyapa and affording me this life so that I may do your work helping these families. Please guide us in our journey as we embrace your light. Amen."

Margoth kept her head bowed and added her own prayer. One that would guide her in a way to help her mother, sister, and her people. "And please give me the strength to be your servant. As the words of Joshua 1:9, have and always will remind me of your will, 'Have I not commanded you? Be strong and courageous. Do not be afraid; do not be discouraged, for the Lord your God will be with you wherever you go.'"

#

Carmen whistled, and the children hurried to a pine tree with their cardboard box piñata hanging from the lower branches. Margoth tied a red cloth around her sister's eyes, handed her a stick, and spun her around. The children clapped their hands, all hoping to get a turn. It made Carmen's day, knowing that she could put something inside the box. She had picked lichas from the roadside and used one of the mangos Margoth bought at the market.

Rosa tended the firepit with one log at a time. Señora Ramon and another neighbor, señora Vega chatted while they pinched tiny bits of their food and nibbled. Three little girls sang songs and swayed their skirts.

Rosa served the young missionary who took a moment to thank her for the dish of food before taking a seat on a log piece by the piñata crowd. He joined in the laughs and cheers with each pass or hit. There were giggles at the misses and claps at the hits. Still the piñata lived on.

The man took a bite of Margoth's tamale. He looked at his plate and then back to Rosa and called, "Señora, this is delicious."

Rosa dipped her head to smile, "Gracias, but you need to tell Margoth. It was her hands that made them."

28 | Jeffrey Hartman

"Really, then I'll be sure to tell her." George continued to savor each bite. He closed his eyes and rolled the savory dish on his tongue.

Margoth saw him on her way to take a try at breaking the piñata. His reaction to her labor brought a newfound joy. She hadn't ever stopped to see if anyone other than her family enjoyed the dish. Now she was intrigued. She wanted to see the smiles and purposely looked at the women and children's faces as she took the stick. Just before Carmen tied the scarf around her eyes, she glimpsed George smile as she closed her lips around her spoon. It filled Margoth's heart with warmth. *How have I never appreciated their joy before?* The young woman took a swing, and the piñata broke.

Nuts and the fruit fell to the ground. Children dropped to their knees to gather the scattered treats. Carmen crawled between Margoth's knees to take a handful and tucked it into the hem of her embroidered skirt. George from MercyLink sprinkled a fistful of butterscotch candies in the pile. Several little boys used cupped hands to scoop up nuts and candy. Each scampering off to share their loot.

Margoth laughed. "Save me one!"

"Certainly," a low male voice assured.

Margoth removed her blindfold. "Oh, I thought I was talking to my sister." She extended her hand to him, "I saw you in town today. I'm Margoth."

"Nice to meet you, Margoth, I'm George." He gave Margoth a butterscotch wrapped in yellow paper and took another from his pocket for himself. "Are all birthdays like this?"

"I don't know about all of Honduras, but here we are all family. Welcome to Honduras, Señor George."

Chapter 3
NEW FRIENDS

New Friends

It had been a week since Margoth met George at Carmen's birthday celebration. His presence enlivened her faith in herself. Margoth decided to seek guidance from her pastor. She prayed for her mother, sister, and their small home daily. She knew God was listening because their home was spared from Hurricane Mitch's wrath, the floods did not affect the little abode. Another sign: she and her sister were spared from the gangs the day before.

Hurricane Mitch came through with a vengeance. The storm stalled over Honduras bringing torrential rains that brought flooding and mudslides which left Margoth's neighbors homeless and jobless. Their abode was a mere 350 sq ft made from concrete blocks, painted yellow with blue flowers on the outside. The hearth and fireplace were intact, and the shrine they kept in the corner remained. Although during the storm's battering they lost the flame, the three women huddled in the center of the home beneath the wooden table. Water rose a foot deep, and the tin roof blew off while they moved the table to the corner furthest from the door. The few belongings and food they had were destroyed.

Before the hurricane made landfall on October 29, 1998, Carmen was in school, and the small house was filled with crosses, a family bible, and a picture of Christ hanging on the fireplace. Although financially poor, many Hondurans would be described as "spiritually rich" as they have so little to be thankful except their faith. Margoth lit the candle when the rain began. As the wind picked up, the door relented and blew back to fly off across their yard. The roof took longer. At first the rain dripped in bursts, an accompaniment to the increasing gusts. Margoth held her mother and sister who kept their hands on the bible keeping it close when the roar of peeling metal reverberated within the concrete walls. Each corrugated tin panel relented in succession.

The rain, as much as four inches an hour, beat down on the women's backs. Hurricane Mitch stalled over Honduras for three days. Still, Margoth, Rosa and Carmen remained huddled in prayer.

#

Exhausted from fear, cold, and hunger, the three women emerged from their concrete bunker squinting into the sunlit blue sky. They smiled despite themselves. The reality of the storm's wrath set in the moment they stood in what was once their yard. The neighbors' houses were gone. A river of mud took out the small wooden shacks and several others in its path. The forest trees were ravished.

Margoth stepped in a mix of mud and debris. Her bare feet, waterlogged and numb, were cut by hidden bits of debris that used to be pieces of homes. She looked around her, and the only structure that remained in her immediate square was her own. Faith had gotten them through, of that Margoth was certain.

In need of food, shelter, and hope, Margoth, Rosa, and Carmen made their way to the church at the top of the hill. It was a mile walk in house bits and mud. But they knew to go to their place of comfort and refuge. It lightened their hearts when they saw the building standing with no visible signs of damage. The sun glinted on the circular stained-glass window beneath the steeple. Several other survivors from Nueva Suyapa were also making their way to their trusted place of worship and hope.

#

Two days after putting their names on the pastor's list, two young North American men appeared at their door. Margoth and Carmen managed to find a piece of tin from someone's home and put it over the doorway for a semblance of security. Though looting was rampant in the small village causing the three women to sleep in shifts. Gangs were no longer the biggest threat. Anyone who had a crumb of food or alcohol was a target. Six women were killed protecting their homes, but for what? Like everyone else, they had nothing. There was no food, no clean water, and only the clothes they re-wore after hanging them to dry on mud laden sticks and twigs.

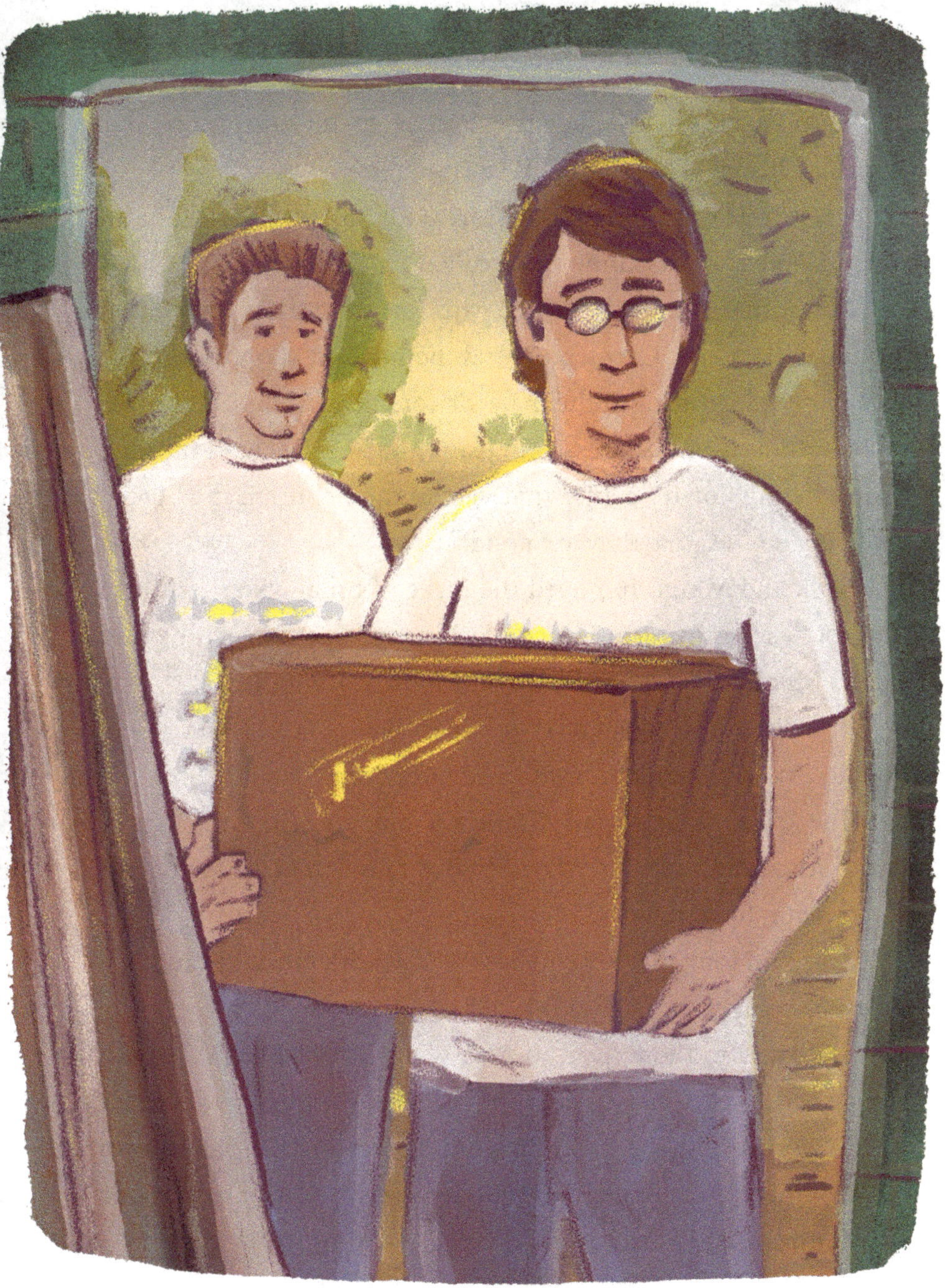

A knock on the tin made the three women freeze. Margoth's heart lay heavy in her chest. "Who's there?"

"Pastor David sent us. We are looking for Ms. Margoth Cruz," A young masculine voice called.

Margoth exchanged a glance with Rosa and the elder woman nodded. They kept Carmen behind them while Margoth slid the tin to the side peering at the male visitors. When she saw the two men in their twenties dressed in jeans and T-shirts with the logo from the missionary center that visited their church, she tucked back inside. "Mama, they are good."

Rosa and Margoth moved the piece of tin and stepped from the roofless home, arm in arm. Still, they kept Carmen behind them. Margoth extended her hand, "I am Margoth Cruz."

The lead young man shook her hand, "Good morning, Ma'am. We are here to fix your roof and door."

The other young man handed a box to Margoth. "There are clothes and food for you and your family. Do we have your permission to start work?"

Margoth took the box and eyes welled with gratitude and joy. "Yes, of course. Thank you."

The men motioned to another who stayed by a cart with construction materials. They brought out a ladder and started with layering new tin on the roof and screwing the panels into place. One man measured the door frame and created a door from lumber and hardware.

Margoth and Rosa stood outside unsure of what to do. There were bananas in the box, so Rosa handed one to Carmen and took the box from Margoth. "Eat, you are hungry." Margoth nodded and took a banana. She ate it quicker than she would have liked because she knew her mother, too, was hungry. She also knew that a box of food in the open, meant everyone around knew they had food and were now fodder for looting. It was unspoken but understood that she would take the box from her mother to keep it safe until they could go back into their home. For her mother to eat, the box had to be secure.

Before the men left, they dug a secure spot in the mud by the house and replaced the old metal can the Cruz family used to collect water with a clean plastic cistern.

#

Two thousand and one and the roof was still holding. Not a leak, and the house was back to a place of comfort. The door was solid and had two chain locks. There had been two subsequent deliveries from Pastor David himself during the year. One was a garbage bag of clothes and a curtain for the one window. The other was a box of food sent by MercyLink.

The women felt blessed by the generosity of people they never met, and rich in faith that the Lord would provide. They also knew that others in their village were less fortunate. Some left homeless moved to the landfill outside Tegucigalpa where they had a chance of structuring a form of shelter from trash scraps and trucks brought recyclables and refuse daily. It was more than they had and with jobs lost to the storm because of destroyed crops and businesses, there was no work which meant no income.

The gangs were worse than they had been. They were thugs that demanded part of the earnings businesses acquired during the day or week. And they looked for women to harass. Margoth knew it was a matter of time before she was confronted, and that day came. She and Carmen were deep in chat when the gang member Margoth had eyed on Carmen's birthday decided she needed to be put in her place. He followed the two women and grabbed Margoth putting her up against the wall. Carmen ran into a shop, but the owner would not help.

When Carmen returned, Margoth had a bloodied lip. "I am to consider myself warned," she said to Carmen. They left for home and hadn't been back to Nueva Suyapa's city center since. Instead, Margoth planned to go to talk with Pastor David. She was determined to make a better life for her family and the women in her village. They had worth and she would show them. On her way up the hill to the church, she recited her favorite verse, *"Have I not commanded you? Be strong and courageous. Do not be afraid; do not be discouraged, for the Lord your God will be with you wherever you go."* At end of her recitation, she reached the steps of the church. At the top were Pastor David, and her new friend George.

The pastor held the door open, his eyes focused on the young woman's lip. "Welcome, Margoth. Please come in."

Chapter 4
INSPIRATION

Inspiration

"My friend George, here, and I were just talking about ways to best serve our little community. And here you are, Margoth. I believe it is fate that brought you here today." Pastor David explained.

"Butterscotch?" George offered.

Margoth took the candy and slipped it between her lips. "Thank you."

"Now, George why don't you fill Margoth in on what we were talking about."

Margoth stood with her back to the wall and savored the buttery sweet treat, delighted to be included in the conversation.

George propped himself against the back of a pew and began. "I was telling, Pastor David, that Honduras is one of the most dangerous places in the world for women." He glanced at Margoth. "The local culture, and the Catholic Church teachings in Honduras, do not favor birth control. It is difficult for women to get birth control assistance, and so this causes a high degree of unwanted pregnancies, particularly when considering that so many of the men could not care less, drink too much, etc.....

Most of the men do not play a role in assisting with help at home of child rearing, and so our programs are focused primarily on helping women."

Margoth nodded in agreement. "You have no idea how true your words are, señor George. Many women in my community have many children and are too malnourished to provide milk for the infants. One lost two children last year because she could not feed them. Her husband left for the United States and promised to send money, but she has yet to hear from him."

George shook his head in acknowledgment and disgust. "Are you aware that 4% of infants born in Honduras die before reaching age five? That's five times the rate in the United States. It is heart wrenching, and please, call me George."

Margoth nodded.

Pastor David added, "I believe your own husband left for the United States and did not return, isn't that so, Margoth?"

"It is," she said, her voice flat. Margoth married at nineteen to a field worker. He harvested sugarcane. After Margoth lost her child to miscarriage, he decided to tell her he was going to find work in the United States to make a better life for them and to afford medical care. He was distraught because the child she lost would have been his son. But after five years, she gave up hope. She realized he either didn't make it or did and forgot about her. Not that he was a loving husband, he was abusive. Having a fat lip from a gang member was not new. The sting and throb were familiar. That was what happened when a husband came home enraged from unfair pay and alcoholic stupors. She had forgotten who she was talking to. She folded her lip in and pulled her braid to cover her mouth.

George glanced at Pastor David and then back to Margoth, "27% of Honduran women have experienced physical or sexual violence at some point in their lives."

"Margoth, you do not have a husband. What happened? Do you wish to talk in private?"

"It's fine. The gang member, I did not cower to, decided to teach me a lesson two days ago. I came to seek your guidance. I have not been back to the city center, but it is not possible to stay away." Margoth confided to her trusted friends. "Domestic violence in Honduras is rampant, and the macho culture does little to stop this. Many husbands are alcoholics or drug users and abusive to their wives. I do not need a husband; I need to learn to take care of myself and teach other women that they too can make a change."

"Then, Margoth, I believe you and George have much to discuss, because my friend has his own plan to help the women in your community. And you are the one who, I believe, has the strength and courage to make it happen."

MARGOTH | 43

Margoth smiled. *God has brought us together this day,* she thought. She did not have much by way of food, but she would be glad to give up her papusa for Pastor David and George if it meant he could help her find a way to bring her dream to life. Though she would give up her papusa just to feed them if they were hungry. She was more fortunate than a lot of the women around her, and lucky enough to have dinner each night, no matter how little. "Pastor David, George, would you like to come to my house for dinner? We can make plans to make my community strong. I want to hear what you have in mind."

Pastor David dipped his head and clutched her hands. "Ah Margoth, I must decline your invitation. I have other obligations, but I am sure George will take you up on your offer."

George smiled, "I would be delighted. I will not come empty handed."

Margoth's chest lightened. She thanked Pastor David and George and bowed her head and left the church with joy in her heart. There was hope and hope was motivation. She was going to listen, learn, and make the difference the women of Nueva Suyapa needed.

#

George knocked on the crafted pine door. Carmen bounded to the door, "Who is it?"

"George, Margoth's friend." George called.

Carmen pulled the door open and let George in. He had a canvas bag in his arms and loaf of bread. Carmen smiled; her eyes focused on the bread. They did not eat bread. They had tortillas and papusa, rice and fruit. But bread was not a part of their regular food and they had not had it since before Hurricane Mitch.

Margoth stood at the table with four papusas, a bit smaller than normal. Rosa had taken a bit of the masa, water, and queso from the three that were to be their dinner and made a fourth. She knew that the amount they missed would not leave them in hunger.

"That smells delicious," George said smiling back at Carmen and then focusing on Margoth, "I brought bread and a gift of rice, beans, and a papaya." He set down a 10-pound bag of rice, 5 of beans and the papaya before handing the loaf of bread Rosa. "Thank you, for inviting me into your home."

"You are a gift from God, señor," Rosa exclaimed.

He smiled.

Rosa prepared the papaya and sliced the bread while Carmen arranged the food on four plates. Margoth filled a mug with water from the cistern and offered it to George. There was one wooden chair that Margoth offered to George and then took a seat on the floor.

George sat on the floor across from her and clasped his knees. "Let's start with what you want to do, Margoth. Then I will tell you how I can help."

Margoth took one of the plates that Carmen brought to the two as they planned. "I used to wonder how I could help. What is my purpose? Now, I believe my purpose is to be a voice for the women of Nueva Suyapa. I want to have my own business where my mother and sister can work and not depend on finding odd jobs."

"That is wonderful, but you said you want to help the women. How will that help them?" George questioned.

Margoth stared at her plate. One small papusa, a piece of bread, a slice of papaya, and a shared cup of water should make her feel the guilt she had brewing in the pit of her stomach. "There are children a few houses over, that have no dinner. As you go toward the capital city of Tegucigalpa, there is a landfill where many of my neighbors go to scrounge for scraps. And I am sitting here with a full plate in my lap, feeling with a heavy heart, George. I want to share my plate with them all, and I can't. I need to eat to help my mother and keep my sister as safe as I can. I don't want my family to go hungrier than they already do. I want to make a change and if that works, teach the other women that they too can change their path." She blinked away unshed tears.

Rosa came over and kissed the top of Margoth's head. "The Lord has made you strong, m'hija."

Carmen knelt beside George and took his hand. She then took her sister's. Margoth joined hands with her mother and George. Rosa took Carmen's and then prayed. "Lord, we thank you for this wonderful food, and our new friend, George. Both are blessings to this home and with your guidance my dear Margoth will do your service. Please guide her in helping the women and children who are less fortunate. And I beg you to continue to keep us all safe. Amen."

George, Carmen, and Margoth repeated, "Amen."

It was quiet while they all pinched pieces of food. Margoth watched George taste the papusa. "Do you like it?"

"I do. You ladies know how to cook."

"If it didn't take a lot of money, I would start my own stand."

George perked up. "Really, and what would you sell?"

"I'm not sure. Papusas are common. I would need to make something people want but won't make. At least not all the time."

"What about the tamales?" George asked. "They were absolutely delicious. The smell of achiote and chicken was enough to make your mouth water. Are they hard to make?"

Rosa smiled at him. "They are not hard, but time consuming and they take a lot of ingredients."

"So, tell me. What are the ingredients? We can review each one and add up how much you would need to sell them in the city center for ten people. We figure out the cost and adjust the amount to accommodate the clientele. If you sell out, then we increase the tamales. If you do not, we need to consider another food option. But cooking is something you know, Margoth. You can use that skill and knowledge to start your business."

Rosa and Carmen cleaned up the dinner plates while Margoth and George went outside to plan. They went over the number of banana leaves, pounds of masa flour, and the whole list of ingredients for a good hearty tamale batch. Water was not readily available, and they needed to account for it.

"I think you should start with a meal price," George suggested.

"What do you mean? I don't have the money to make more food."

"I mean, that you can charge $4 for a tamale with a drink. That drink can be coconut milk, juice, or bottled water. You can offer just one for now. As your business grows so will your options, but it is convenient when you get a meal to have a drink handy."

"How will I ever get the money to do this? There is so much." Margoth rested her head in her hands.

George sat with his back against the side of the concrete house. "I never told you why I came to Honduras, Margoth."

The young entrepreneur looked up.

"I am here to help women like you get started. To guide you in creating a livable wage and assisting you with the costs of that start up. We call them micro-loans. We provide you with business information and training, as well as guidance in financial planning to get you started."

Margoth knew then, that God had afforded her the opportunity she prayed for. It was up to her to make it work. For the first time, she took a deep breath and sighed with hope for her and the women of Nueva Suyapa's future.

"Let's do this, señor George."

Chapter 5
2002 OPENING DAY

52 | Jeffrey Hartman

2002 Opening Day

"Pray for me, mama," Margoth called as she and Carmen left with a box full of tamales. Each was wrapped in a banana leaf ready to keep warm in a pushcart steamer.

The cart was an investment, George explained. He provided Margoth with a micro-loan of $500 to get a pushcart and enough supplies to make saleable food. She used pork for the tamales, purchased more masa flour and spices, in hope of selling her first batch. She wanted to sell ten, but George talked her into making 20 and providing a bottle of water with each. Margoth loaded the cart and set off for the city Centre.

#

Margoth and Carmen pushed the cart over the rough streets. There were potholes and pebbles in the asphalt. When they reached the city itself, Margoth searched for the spot in front of a tobacco store. George made certain that she had her papers from the City Council and a signed document giving her permission to park her cart. In exchange, she would give 1% of her daily profit. The document would expire in six months, because George did not want her to be indebted to the shop owner and told her it gave her a way out if the business failed.

She parked the cart in front and lit the tiny gas burner to heat the water and keep the food hot. Carmen grabbed the paper plates and plastic forks from a small compartment underneath. The moment Margoth had dreamed of was at hand. She was a businesswoman, even in her worn pink blouse and white pants. She pulled out a poster board and wrote in large letters: TAMALES Y AGUA $3

Her hand shook. Many people lived on a dollar a day or less. Most wished for six, but in the city Centre, there were officials, and business owners. George told her about investing money to make money. And that to bring in a profit she had to find buyers.

The church bell struck, and it was noon. A handful of businessmen passed her by without a look. Another hour passed. Still no customers. Rather than be discouraged, Margoth recited, "Have I not commanded you? Be strong and courageous. Do not be afraid; do not be discouraged, for the Lord your God will be with you wherever you go."

As she finished reciting, Pastor David walked up to Margoth's cart. "Margoth! Are these the infamous tamales George told me about?"

"They are indeed," she said, smiling at Carmen.

"Then I will take one. I heard they are hard to resist." The pastor handed his money to Margoth.

She put it in a little bag made from an old sock and tucked it in her blouse. She took a tamale from the steamer and removed the filling from the banana leaf. It filled a third of the plate. The smell emanated around the stand, and she grabbed a bottle of water from a box below.

Two men walking by, stopped to read Margoth's sign as she handed the plate to Pastor David. The pastor took a bite and closed his eyes. "Margoth, this is fantastic. George wasn't kidding. The flavor…." He took another bite and shook his head. "Wonderful, thank you."

Margoth smiled.

"We'll take two," said one of the stopped men. He handed Margoth the money and she stuffed it in a crevice of the cart.

She did the same, process: unwrap the tamales, and slide them onto the plate, and she handed the meals to the two men. "Thank you, please enjoy."

The man who remained silent, took a bite, and covered his lips with the back of his hand. "This is the food of Honduras." He took a bigger second bite.

His friend tried his and nodded at Margoth. "Will you be back tomorrow?"

"I will," she said.

"Good, I want my colleagues to taste these. You are a wonderful cook."

Before the men left another group approached. Each ordered one meal. Each showed enjoyment, to Margoth's delight. By four o'clock she was sold out. She bundled up the box she had the waters in and turned off the burner. She kept the water in the steamer for washing the cart later and set off for home with Carmen. The two women chatting in their excitement.

Margoth kept a look out for the gangs and kept her head down. Though she was happy, she did not want to draw attention to herself. For the first time in her life, she held sixty dollars. *If the same happens tomorrow, I will be able to pay back George and keep food in my mama and sister's bellies,* she thought.

#

Margoth parked the cart in front of the house. She took the empty cardboard boxes in the house. Rosa was at the table counting banana leaves.

"Margoth, did they sell?" Rosa asked, the empty boxes drawing her attention.

"Not only did they sell, mama, a few people asked if I would be back again tomorrow."

"Oh, thank you, Lord, for giving my daughter this opportunity," Rosa prayed as she hugged Margoth.

"Isn't George supposed to check in tonight?" Carmen asked.

"He is," Margoth affirmed.

George had promised to see how the first day went, and to go over the plan if it needed an adjustment. Margoth decided to make a plan for when he arrived. She looked at the box and decided that with the money she made, she could get pork for the red masa tonight. She could then make the dough and wrap it before leaving in the late morning. She would be there sooner, and now that the people knew where she was, there may be more requests. She would check with George, but she was certain an increase to twenty-five tamales would be a safe inventory.

Margoth took the money sock from her blouse and checked the crevice of the cart before taking a small amount to go back in town for the meat and water. As she was leaving, George stepped into her yard.

"Back home so soon?" He asked. "Is that a good sign?"

Margoth smiled in spite of herself. "I sold them all, and now I have to go get more meat."

"May I walk with you?" he asked.

Fear is a constant companion for a woman walking the streets at dusk in Nueva Suyapa, and so Margoth welcomed Geroge's company. "That would be appreciated. You're a good friend, George. Why do you go to so much trouble to help others, especially strangers that live in another part of the world?" asked Margoth.

"You are also a good friend, Margoth. I believe we have an imperative to 'Love our neighbors', and neighbors can be someone that lives right next door, or thousands of miles away. I also believe that 'Faith without action is dead', and true believers are called to put their faith into action. By helping you and these other women, I feel I am fulfilling that mandate. It's very important to how I live my life. It's about more than me. It's about what I can help others do. And, not to change the subject, I just may have to stop by and get one of the pork tamales tomorrow. I tasted the chicken and need to experience the pork."

"Then I will save one for you."

"Thank you."

#

Margoth managed to sell off her inventory the next day. She had enough money to buy her supplies on the way home and even paid the tobacco shop owner. Her newly-discovered business acumen was invigorating. She had planned to see George in a week to let him know the progress and to work out the first loan payment. As an experiment, she decided to add another five tamales each day, until she reached a limit that no longer sold.

Rosa stood by the table with a stack of banana leaves. She prepared them the day before so that the masa could be made fresh, and the leaves were ready for filling. The women put the meat in a pot on the fire and let it stew overnight for the red masa. They even had enough leftover so that they could eat a bit of pork for breakfast with a tortilla. It was more than they could have hoped for.

"God is good," Carmen said.

"He provides," Margoth assured. "I will wait the six months for my documents to renew before consulting George, but I want to focus on opening my own shop. I don't want to sell on the street where the gangs come through. It is only a matter of time before they harass me. They always harass the business owners."

"And a shop will change that?" Carmen asked.

"No, but it will give us shelter."

Margoth washed the steamer and used the water for the two new chickens she brought home. In time they would have eggs again. There was light in her life. She found her calling. The Microfinance loan, and the initial training had inspired Margoth to believe she could achieve her goals and succeed. She felt empowered. Her mind was transformed. She wrote down every chore and act to ensure other women would learn from her own journey. Obtaining the documents was easy with George, and new ministry members were due to arrive any day. She was excited and wanted to meet with them. One was a woman by the name of Margaret who was starting a bible study for women like Margoth. George had invited Margoth on the way to buy meat. It was all Margoth could think of; other women who succeeded.

The rain pattered against the secured tin roof. Hurricane season was still three months off, so the three women secured the door, bringing the chickens inside.

"I won't lose these to those wild dogs, again," Margoth declared. "We need the eggs." Then she had an idea. "If I buy enough chickens, in six months I can sell the eggs at the shop. We can sell eggs from home or keep them to eat."

Rosa kissed Margoth's cheek. "I love you, my smart strong girl."

Chapter 6
SPRING 2002

Spring 2002

"Six months went by faster than I realized," Margoth said to George who was sitting on a wooden chair at the table inside the little concrete house. It was a purchase Margoth was willing to splurge on because she wanted her mother to have a place to sit. It was the first big purchase and the first chair they had since Hurricane Mitch destroyed their belongings.

"Congratulations, Margoth." He handed her another document, but this one had: Paid in Full written on the top. Margoth had paid back the micro loan of $500 in just six months. "You ready to take on a full shop?"

"I am. I have my mother and sister to help. We will have a refrigerator and running water. If all goes well, I can start to reach out to the other women. And there is a young boy that comes around, an orphan. I have him doing errands for me in exchange for one tamale. I am thinking of taking him in at the shop. He used to live at the Tegucigalpa Landfill. Now he lives on the streets here in Nueva Suyapa. He walked over three miles to get here."

"What made him come?" George asked.

Margoth sighed, "His mother and father died at the landfill. They had dysentery. He can't be more than eight and can't read or write."

"Margoth, you know the children pick through the trash for fifty cents per day to try to live. Some of them are orphans, some of those kids working at the landfill sniff glue in order to get high…just to get through the day, and to try to disguise the horrible smell of the methane that is a constant reality near the landfill. Some of the girls, that pick through the trash, are so desperate they offer to spend private time - for money- with the truck drivers that are delivering trash to the landfill."

Margoth nibbled on a tortilla and sipped a cup of water from the cistern. "I know. It breaks my heart. He walked into the city Centre a few months back. His legs were like sticks. Having my food has brought back a light in his eyes, but I can't feed all the children. Not yet."

"Margoth, you can't do it all at once. It takes time. Kids in Honduras suffer from chronic malnutrition, because their diet is lacking in fresh fruits and vegetables. They suffer from brain damage, learning difficulties, and stunted development because they lack Iron, Iodine, and other nutrients. You can't fix it all. But you can help them learn to change the way they live by teaching your gift."

"Gift?"

"Yes, the gift of business knowledge. You became a success from the first day because you did not give up. You are fierce and strong. Many of these women are not. Or at least they don't believe they have it in them to be."

Margoth smiled. "Then I need to get this shop open. What a better way, to help my neighbors, I will teach them how to work."

There was one neighbor that Margoth thought about. Señora Ramon was a mother with three living children, and one on the way. She had attended Carmen's birthday celebration. A woman who lost two children to illnesses related to malnutrition, she was determined to change her situation. If there was any woman that Margoth wanted to start helping, it was her.

"George, I know what I am going to do," she declared after her reflection. "I will expand my micro-business with Ines Ramon."

George nodded, smiling. "Margoth, I am blessed to have met you. Your faith, love, and determination are an inspiration to us all. Why don't you bring your friend with you to the next bible study? We have a new family of missionaries arriving this afternoon. Tomorrow is the meeting. Bring her along, and we'll have a box of supplies for her. Tell me what she needs."

"She has a baby on the way, and three children from two years to seven. Any food you can offer will give her peace. Clothes are good, but food is needed to live. If you give her money her husband will take it. Tomorrow, I'll talk to her."

#

Margoth had her tamale cart parked inside the shop. She planned to sell them from the cart until the store was cleaned and set up for business but wanted to draw her faithful customers to her new location a few windows down on the same block. She propped the door open and set the cart against the front window. She tied her handmade posterboard sign to the door with twine. Still, the tamale meal was $3. She hoped the added menu items would allow her to keep the prices low. But she had new expenses. There were utility bills, taxes, and rent. She liked having the cart, but customers were inquiring about other dishes. She needed the bigger place. After paying the electric company, she found a used refrigerator that another shop owner had thrown away. She salvaged it and put the next day's meat inside along with a bowl of eggs she collected from her chickens. In time, she hoped to add many more chickens to her beginning flock. Rosa brought a bowl of beans that she cooked overnight, and another with rice cooked with coconut milk. Carmen and the orphaned boy, named Juan, carried them.

Juan put the bowl of cooked rice on the floor by a wooden counter that was attached to the back wall. The store had been a tailor shop, but the businessman died. The table and counter were left behind. Along with a lamp and several piles of cloth. The landlord was going to dispose of it all. Margoth jumped on the chance and asked if she could have it all. To her surprise he affirmed but charged her $10 for the lot. She planned to put Rosa to work, making curtains and tablecloths.

As the women and orphan cleaned, Margoth's regulars came to check out the new place. For an added $1, an opening day special, they could get beans and rice with their tamale. George showed up with Pastor David and several new faces wearing matching white polo shirts.

"Hola!" George called as the troop entered the shop.

"Hello, my friend," Margoth greeted. She went to the group. "I'm Margoth. I thought I was going to meet you all tonight."

"They just arrived, and I thought it would be a warm welcome to introduce them to our newest entrepreneur.". And of course, a warm Honduran meal is a good welcome too," George laughed.

"I believe we will all take today's special," Pastor David said, reading the added section on the old, tattered sign.

"Thank you," Margoth said; her eyes twinkled in the light from tears. Though she was already happy and was not sad, she felt an overwhelming sensation. It welled in her eyes and took the breath from her chest. "Tonight, I will bring my friend Ines Ramon."

Pastor David clasped her hands, "I look forward to meeting with you both."

The bible study was a welcome and popular refuge for the women of Margoth's community. A different kind of study than discussing the verses and the application to their lives and acceptance to the Holy Spirit. Instead, they discussed the women in the bible and their strengths. They learned how to apply their skills to do God's work, helping and serving those less fortunate. For all the women in the group had known harder times. Spending time in God's word was nourishment to their souls. They were making a change.

Margoth dished the food while Carmen handed the plates to the group. After the last was served, they left to eat in the city Centre. Margoth was up to fifty tamales per day. She thought lessening that in the days to come would help her pay for the costs of other dishes. Her mother would make empanadas and papusas while Carmen took orders. If Ines was willing, she would teach her how to use her skills and sell them. She would even show her how to get documents. And if she needed, help her apply for a micro loan.

#

The time had come for the door to close. Rosa, Carmen, and Juan loaded the cart with empty bowls and utensils that needed to be cleaned and refilled the next morning. Margoth gathered the money and secured the door. They had sold all the beans and rice with the tamales. But instead of going home to make dinner, Margoth set aside a meal setting for each of them. They worked hard for what they had, and the food was left from the day. Four tamales and four waters with a dollop of rice and a ladle of beans split four ways was more food than any of them were used to. They had food in the cart ready to eat.

When they arrived at the house, Margoth gave Juan a spoon and encouraged him to bow his head for grace before they ate. Juan had slept on the street for months. He had no shelter and ducked under whatever cover he found, even an empty bench was better than being pelted by the rain, full on. Margoth discussed her sadness for the boy with Pastor David who encouraged her to speak with her mother and sister before bringing him into her home.

"You don't know this boy, Margoth. Taking him in, will mean adding a responsibility. Are you sure you have the means to do that?"

"I cannot pay him, but I can feed him. Give him a corner to sleep in under a roof. It's better than wondering when I won't see him; knowing in my heart that I could have saved him."

"Pray on it, Margoth. And if your heart still yearns to help the boy, then bring it to your mother and sister. For taking in an orphan of his age will change life for all of you. He has to go to school, you have no papers for him, he needs clothes, and your business is still new."

Margoth presented the idea of taking Juan into their home to her mother and sister. Rosa was against it. They had gotten out of near-starvation and desperate poverty only a couple months prior. She did not feel that they were ready to add the responsibility, but she did invite George to come talk with them because she did not want to see ill come to the boy.

MARGOTH | 69

When George came to visit, Margoth told him the story. "I saw him huddled between the buildings. His legs were sticks; his eyes half closed from hunger. The hair on his head was dull. He didn't ask me for food. Instead, he asked me if he could help me so he could buy food. I asked him how much he wanted, and he said, 'Someday I want to make fifty cents a day. But I won't ask you to pay me that.'" Margoth laughed, "I told him I had a lot of work to do, and he said he wanted to work."

"Instead of begging, he offered himself to work." George acknowledged. "And that is why you feel for him. He wants to earn his way. That is commendable, Margoth."

"He is different. I believe I can teach him to help others and change his status," she admitted.

"Can't the mission help him? Provide him an education?" Rosa asked.

"I'll look into it, but there are a lot of children like Juan."

"Thank you," Margoth said.

Six months later Juan was staying in the house at night and doing all the jobs Rosa, Carmen, and Margoth needed. He brought water from the cistern into the house, cleaned the fireplace, and brought in wood. Carmen taught him to clean the chickens and had him help keep them in the yard, safe from wild dogs. She also showed him how to pick lichas. Without realizing her role, Margoth had already taken on her first student. She was teaching a boy with nothing how to become something, and to share the fruits of his labor with others in need.

Chapter 7
INJUSTICE

72 | Jeffrey Hartman

Injustice

The sun beat down on the asphalt street. A bag of rice lay spilled on the sidewalk. Margoth screamed, "Carmen es Mama."

Carmen pulled the curtain back to see what was wrong. The inflection of her sister's voice rose the hairs on her arms. "Que es?" Her voice caught in fear. Rosa was not there. "Mama, mama!"

Carmen opened the cafe door. "Hermanita! Where is our mother?" She ran from the shop. "Where is she? What happened?" The younger woman ran to Margoth headfirst. She buried her face in the white linen shirt decorated with vibrant embroidered flowers drowning the delicate thread with her tears, when she spotted the listless form.

"They shot her."

"Who?" Carmen asked.

"The same ones that wanted money last week, Carlos' gang." Margoth cried. The dust on her smooth tanned face gleamed with tears. "I heard shots and she fell." The woman drew in a deeper breath and sobbed.

Margoth pulled Rosa into her chest. Her mother coughed; her eyes stared at her daughter. "Mama, no. Come, we will go to the hospital. Carmen, we need George or Pastor David."

The two women huddled where Rosa lay, blood seeped through her T-shirt. The older woman had worn a pair of jeans with a white T-shirt and rubber sandals. Margoth always taught the women to carry a knife and stay alert. Regardless, they were in a street with frequent gang visits. Violence against women was still rampant. That had not changed.

"My sweet girls," Rosa breathed.

"Shhh," Margoth whispered and kissed the woman's head. Losing her mother to gang violence, seemed surreal. She now understood the fear and ache in Carmen's chest when she lost her father. It was hard to escape the gut-wrenching guilt which weighed on her heart. Margoth knew there was no use yelling Rosa's name. If she was shot twice, there was little chance that she would survive. Margoth could only pray that her mother would pass quickly.

A death at the hands of bullying men, traffickers, drug lords, and ill-intentioned thugs was not kind to the many women and girls who disappeared. Most were never found, dead or alive. Honduras is one of the deadliest places in the world to be a woman, where so many crimes against women are simply not investigated.

Margoth closed her eyes, "Carmen, say with me, 'Have I not commanded you? Be strong and courageous. Do not be afraid; do not be discouraged, for the Lord your God will be with you wherever you go.'" The two women whispered the words. A vindication for them, but a reminder for Rosa whose breath labored. "Be strong, Mama, you must."

Margoth shook her head. "When happiness had filled my heart, and my family was fed, someone had to bring back the pain."

Carmen sobbed. "We can't go to the police; they won't care that mama's dying. Maybe if they got their head out of the bottle and kept their noses clean from dope, they would remember that women were once their mothers…the mothers of their children." The embittered words were clear.

Margoth scanned the streets for a glimpse of someone, anyone. The people always disappeared when shots rang. Carmen rocked Rosa's lifeless body. Margoth tried anyway. She stepped into the street and called, "Ayudame, por favor, ayudame." She dropped to her knees; the blazing sun burned her skin. She reached down to touch the drying crimson puddle. The church bell rang, and Margoth knew that her mama, was gone.

#

The shops of Nueva Suyapa were prey to the street thugs. Gangs that wanted money in exchange for a week without violence. They would bully their way into the shops and threaten the owners at gunpoint. Too many resisted Carlos's gang and met the same fate as Rosa. But Margoth hadn't resisted. Carmen and Rosa knew to hand his gang the envelope with the week's dues. Margoth called them dues since she had to pay them to have peace. It was always on a Friday when Carlos came round to collect. This was Wednesday.

Margoth's wails brought curious eyes from the neighboring shop windows. The streets cleared except for one businessman on his way to get his regular order of tamales with a side of beans and rice from Margoth's café. He spotted the three women on the sidewalk.

"Girls, I'm so sorry," he said. "It wasn't Carlos," the man said.

"How do you know?" Margoth hissed.

"Carlos is known for one shot to the head. This is a message. I'd say Carlos has a rival. It's a territory war. One wants what the other has. Your guy has the higher end businesses, a good location, and steady pay. Perhaps the other wants in."

A siren sounded in the distance. The sisters held their mother tighter. It was the last chance they would have before the ambulance arrived to take her from them. Margoth scanned the street again, and several people had gathered around them. She wondered who had called. When gangs are present, many are reluctant to get involved with another's misfortune. It wasn't because they didn't care, she knew that. It was because they feared the repercussions. The blatant cold- blooded attacks on those trying to help a neighbor.

#

The ambulance pulled next to the sidewalk. The two women clung to their mother. Two men in blue uniforms opened the back and brought out the gurney. Margoth urged her sister to step back. "Carmen, we have to let her go."

"No, I won't," the sixteen-year-old cried.

Margoth crouched beside her and helped lower their mother to the pavement. "She is already with God. Come." It made the older sister's heart ache to hold her sister as their mother was covered with a white sheet and loaded into the back of the ambulance. Margoth didn't want to be the strong one. She was tired and wanted to cry. But she had a shop to close for the day, and food to prepare for the next day. Because a gang war wasn't going to shut her down.

Juan ran from around the corner. He was bringing banana leaves from the market. He spotted the ambulance driving away with Margoth embracing Carmen. "Margoth?"

"Mama's gone, bendito." She opened her arms for the boy to join them. He ran past her into the shop and placed the banana leaves on the table. When he came back out, he picked up the bag of rice, trying to save as much as he could and placed it inside the door. "Gracias, Juan."

Instead of being embraced, he chose to embrace them. He wrapped his little arms around their middles. *"Blessed are those who mourn, for they will be comforted,"* (Matthew 5:4. 4). He kissed both their cheeks and pulled them into the shop.

Chapter 8
RESISTANCE

Resistance

"Margoth, is there anything I can do for you and your sister," George asked.

"You've done more than enough George. Mama is gone because of greed. All those men want is money and they will do anything to get what little we have. My shop is small. I am one woman with a sister who makes lunch for businessmen. They do not need my $6 a week, but I give it to them. And they kill my mother anyway." Margoth blotted the tears on her cheeks.

She was done sobbing. Her mother was laid to rest in the cemetery at the top of the hill by Pastor David's church. George and the mission took up a fundraiser to offset the funeral cost.

"What will you do now?" George asked. His eyes were focused on Margoth, the concern was more about her livelihood than taking over the household. He knew the conditions Margoth endured. "I don't want to see you give up all your hard work."

"What are you talking about? I'm not giving up anything. If those men think that they can scare me off, then they are mistaken. The Lord has given me strength to endure. I know he walks beside me. Mama is with him. What kind of message would it be if they saw me give up? No, I am here to stay. George, I'm not only staying, but I'm also going to open another café, a large place. I'm going to see what I can afford in Tegucigalpa. Those thugs did not scare me away, they gave me the motivation to be more successful."

George pursed his lips and furrowed his brows. "Margoth, I don't want to see anything happen to you or Carmen. Be careful."

"Thank you, George." Margoth headed to her sister who was talking with Pastor David. "Carmen, we have tamales to make. Mama did not die for us to run and hide. We are strong."

Carmen smiled, a weak straightening of lips. "Did you tell George about your plan for the capital city?"

"I did," Margoth affirmed.

"I want to call it Rosa's."

"I like that, hermana."

The two women descended the hill to their small concrete house. Juan was in school, but they would take him to Rosa's grave after church on Sunday.

#

Margoth recalled, the previous evening; the night their mother passed away; Pastor David came to the house. Juan was sleeping in the corner on a mat with an alpaca blanket. Margoth had Carmen pack the cooked tamales in bags. There were over two dozen that they brought home. Juan suggested they go door to door informing their neighbors of Rosa's passing.

"Margoth," Juan said. "I know the kids are hungry. Maybe we can give them dinner."

"Mama always made sure people had something, even if it was not enough. She went without too often." Carmen reminded.

"Then we feed mom's and kids." Margoth patted Juan's head. "You're a good boy, Juan. Don't let the gangs lure you in."

"They won't. I talked to Pastor David and George. I want to be like them. I like going to school and learning."

The three went around the small community giving out food and telling them their sad news. Most of the women cried out of fear. Rosa was loved, but her death brought the violence to their secluded corner. Nueva Suyapa was just around the bend.

#

"You girls have a plan for him?" Pastor David asked.

Margoth glanced at Carmen. "No, but I don't want to see him in a gang."

The pastor blotted his head with a handkerchief and pulled out a brochure. He opened the trifold document and handed it to Margoth. Children sitting in a group with smiles on their faces was the front-page picture. Inside there were pictures of lunch trays and racks with shoes on them.

"What is this?" Margoth asked.

"This is the ministry and school a small way from here. They take in children in need. The children live in small group homes with married missionary couples from the United States. They raise coffee at their nearby farm. The ministry is called Rancho Elijah. I spoke to them about Juan, and they are willing to take him in. If they do, he will have shoes, food, a bed, and an education that can lead to a college degree. He's a bright lad with big dreams. I don't know if he told you, but he wants to be a pastor. I'd like to give him every chance to succeed. If it is God's will, this may be the path to make it happen."

Carmen squeezed Margoth's arm. "We can get one of the ladies to work with us. We can't let those thugs take him. They'll ruin him."

"I agree. But how do we tell him? I want him to know he is always welcome here, but he has to make something of himself if he wants to help our people." Margoth glanced back at the eight-year-old's lanky form. "He needs more than we can give him here. I'm fighting a battle he doesn't need to be a part of."

#

Morning came, and the two women packed buckets of meat from their iron pot for the tamales. Juan combed his hair and washed his face with a cloth wet from his cup of water. Carmen gave him a tortilla with cheese and a sprinkle of salt. She put a banana next to it.

"Eat them both, you are growing strong, Juan."

He smiled and bit the tortilla. While he chewed, he set it on a blue ceramic plate that Rosa had designated his. "I miss Rosa."

84 | Jeffrey Hartman

"We do too, bendito."

"Knock, knock." A male voice called from the door.

"George!" Juan ran to the door to let the man in. "Why are you here this early?"

Margoth wiped her hands on her apron. Carmen took her place by her sister's side. They exchanged a look that questioned and acknowledged the previous night's conversation.

"I didn't think Pastor David would act so soon." Carmen twisted the cleaning rag she had used to wipe the table.

"When it comes to a good education, it is never too early. Right, Juan?"

Juan finished his tortilla and nodded his head.

"We haven't had a chance to talk to him about our discussion with the pastor," Margoth said.

George folded his lip. They weren't prepared to lose another member of the house in less than two days. They knew the boy would be in a better place, but it didn't make circumstance easier.

"Juan," George whispered. "Remember when you told Pastor David and I that you wanted to be a pastor, too?"

Juan nodded.

"While we can't make that happen, we can put you on the path to take you there, if God wills it. Would you like that?"

Juan glanced at Margoth.

"We don't want the gangs to get to you, Juan. We want you to grow up, maybe go to college, and help people like you want.

Pastor David came here last night and told us about Rancho Elijah. I believe you already know about it. Our door is always open for you." Margoth pulled the boy's head to her chest. "You are like the son I never got to see grow. It would make me proud to be a part of your success."

Carmen kissed his head and cradled his cheek. "I want you to do this. Go prove that change is real."

Juan smiled at George and then back to Margoth and Carmen. "If I go, they won't have me anymore to help them. Who will keep them safe?"

George smiled back. "You are not leaving them. Juan, when you are an educated man, you will help them in ways you do not know. Are you in?"

Margoth winked at him. "You can do this, Juan."

Juan took George's hand. "I think I've been ready. It's what I'm meant to do. I want to go to school, and learn to read, and I will get my own Bible."

Margoth and Carmen wrapped their arms around him. The two saved him from the streets and now they were saving him from the gangs that recruited any way they could. The life of a thug was not one of poverty. They had food. For Juan to seek salvation and education over greed and fear mongering, it was a remarkable choice.

George wrapped his fingers around the boy's hand and led

him out of the small yard, and up the hill toward the church where Juan would find his new home, and a future.

Chapter 9
OVERCOMING

Overcoming

Five years past since Margoth and Carmen lost their mother. As they knew, the gunmen were never sought. But it did not slow the wheels of progress for Margoth. Margoth held Teresa's hand. The woman's daughter, Ana, was a courageous young mother herself. She was a transplant from the Tegucigalpa Landfill. The ministry project there helped the squatters find recyclables. Teresa collected discarded garments such as purses, shoes, clothes, and upholstery. Ana and her sister Paola stripped the fabric from frames, molds, and freed them of buckles or embellishments. They kept rhinestones and buckles to reuse. The missions supported each other. When the project at Tegucigalpa heard from Pastor David that Margoth wanted to change the lives of all women in Nueva Suyapa, they told him about Teresa. The woman kept a large bag of fabric, ready to use. It had no value at the recycling facilities. But to Teresa it was treasure.

Margoth spread the message—her message— of hope and courage to every woman she knew. The small plot of land between hers and the neighbors became a meeting place for nine impoverished women, each with a gift of their own. Teresa had a love for fashion. One would not look at the once skinny woman with big brown eyes, dirty jeans and sneakers worn through the soles and consider her gift was in the fabric arts. But she loved the clothes she found and kept them. Teresa was the first woman Margoth took on as a business prodigy. She had neighbor women to pull rocks from the soil to grow beans and there was enough land to grow food for the four little houses, but she had not noticed anyone with a particular gift.

When Teresa was picking through the landfill four years back, Margoth came to the ministry to learn their mission. She was curious because her new restaurant was open, and it made her think of Juan. He was a vagrant orphan when she started her cart and then he was the first taster when the café opened in Nueva Suyapa. Now he was growing into a fine young man at the seminary. He regularly emailed and texted Margoth. Margoth was shocked at how much more productive she was with the smart phone her business profits afforded her. It made her sad not having him there for opening day. But she thought if he could be saved from the landfill, perhaps there were others, even the women who struggled to survive after Hurricane Mitch. That's when she spotted Teresa. She was one of the women who left after her home was buried in a mudslide, a stone's throw from Margoth's own house.

"Teresa?" Margoth called.

The woman looked up from her treasure hunt. "Margoth?" She gathered her pile of clothing and went to Margoth. "You look good."

Margoth had black slacks and a white blouse and red jacket. "Gracias. Where are the children?" She knew the woman had two and no husband. Marriage wasn't always the way in their part of the world.

"Ana, Paola!" the woman yelled. "They'll come. What are you doing here?"

"Answering a call." Margoth smiled.

Teresa looked at her, confused.

"Come back to Nueva Suyapa with me. You and the girls. I've started a co-op with the women in our neighborhood. I know you have been here for three years, and life won't get easier. God willing, I may be able to change that, Teresa. I want to show you and your daughters how to make a life for yourselves. One where you don't have to go to bed hungry or worry about shelter."

"Margoth," the tired woman breathed. "Where would we stay? I know the landfill."

Margoth wept, controlled but deep. "Look at your girls. Is this the life you want for them? Paola is fifteen years old offering herself to the truck drivers as we speak. I know this is not what you want." Margoth turned away from the young girl who was talking to a driver. "Call her here. I'll give you dinner and a place to stay until you can afford your own. You and the girls. Grab your things if you have some."

"But all the clothes and bags. I can't leave them."

"Show me," Margoth soothed.

"Paola and Ana, ven aca." The girls listened to their mother and hurried toward where she and Margoth stood. "Do you remember Margoth?"

Both girls nodded their heads.

"I am taking the three of you back to Nueva Suyapa. You don't have to sell yourself for food and dig through garbage," Margoth implored. The tears had dried in salted lines on her cheeks. "When I look at you girls I think of my sister. You are beautiful, strong women. You don't need to live like this."

The girls stood behind their mother with hope alight in their eyes. "I know you remember what it felt like to have a home with a fireplace, four walls, and roof," Teresa said to them. "But we do not have enough to eat for a day, Margoth." The woman ducked into a heap of cardboard that turned out to be their shelter. She had an arm full of textiles and slung a suede bag over her shoulder. It had embroidery and beads along the edge. "This is all I have."

"It is a shame what some people throw away. That purse is beautiful. You're lucky to have found it." Margoth couldn't resist looking at the bright thread and rich rusted brown suede.

"Mama didn't find it," Paola said. "She made it."

"You made this?" Margoth gasped. "It's beautiful. People would buy these, Teresa."

"No one wants a bag made from trash." The woman smiled, revealing missing teeth and receding gums. She was malnourished.

94 | Jeffrey Hartman

"Do you have more?" Margoth asked.

"We each have one," Ana said.

"I want you to bring all your gathered clothes and whatnots. Put them in my car." Margoth headed to a 1999 Nissan Sentra. It was her first car and the one that she earned her driver's license in a few months prior to her visit. She used the cart in the Nueva Suyapa shop to sell tamales in Tegucigalpa until she had enough saved to open the restaurant. When her customers heard she offered beans and rice, they started placing orders for the next day. There was more profit to be made in the bigger city.

"You have a car?" Teresa asked.

"I do. Come on, you have a business to plan."

The four women piled into the white Nissan and headed three and a half miles to the outskirts of Nueva Suyapa where Margoth still had her little concrete abode. It was just her and Carmen. There would be plenty of floor space. Since Ana and Paola were too old to go to school, Margoth would teach them how to work with their mother to make a successful business, and she would arrange a micro loan from MercyLink for Teresa.

#

Margoth stood in the entrance of her little house after reminiscing what was the beginning of a community cooperative. She had to leave for her restaurant which now had two employees and sold Teresa's and the women's recycled fabric goods. Margoth loaded her car each day with bags, purses, keychains, and embroidered blouses. She had a window where she displayed the hand-sewn items.

In the late afternoons, Margoth closed her restaurant. As a single woman, not yet thirty, she felt vulnerable. She would bring food that couldn't be save with her to the co-op. The women would feed their children and themselves. Many times, Margoth brought home meat since the restaurant offered more than tamales. They had empanadas and tortillas among other traditional foods. Tegucigalpa, unlike Nueva Suyapa, was a 400-year-old city with stone streets. It was modern and buzzing with people. The crime was still high, but it was worth Margoth's effort to open her business in the heart of it all. Her yellow storefront and large pane glass windows enticed hungry passersby.

She had tables and chairs, though mismatched, and a painting Carmen made before she went to live with one of the businessmen who was a regular over the year. She was just eighteen and thought she loved him. As she had with Juan, Margoth reminded her sister that wherever she lived, Carmen would always be welcome. But that remained true for all the women she helped. Her house was small, but it was a sturdy building.

George had gone back to the United States the month after Rosa's death. He and Margoth stayed in touch through emails and a popular texting app, but the more involved Margoth became with the businesses and recruiting new Microfinance loan candidates, the less time she had to write. Though in one of his messages he did say that he planned to return to Honduras and continue providing micro loans with Margoth's help. George had come to depend on Margoth and the local pastors eye for character as they recruited new micro-business prospects for funding by MercyLink.

#

The women had gone back to their homes. Carmen was running the shop in Nueva Suyapa, so Margoth only visited a few times a week. She sat with Teresa, Ana, and Paola, who was now twenty, washing discarded clothes they got from donations and the landfill. They also traveled into the city sometimes to buy used clothing, which they laundered and repaired, re-selling at a profit. With the nine women working the land, stripping, cleaning, and creating. There wasn't a lot of inventory. Teresa could make a bag in two days. Ana and Paola worked faster, but their stitching wasn't as neat. The girls settled on a pile of blankets and held their plates full of beans and rice with a papusa. Teresa and Margoth sat at the table with their plates. Instead of papusas, they had empanadas. Ana's daughter ate beans, rice, and a tortilla. There was plenty so they each chose their favorites. In four years, the girls blossomed. Teresa gained curves and no longer gave up her food for her daughters. They ate two meals a day, together. Breakfast was on the go. Mostly fruit, but mornings were busy loading Margoth's car and feeding the chickens.

A knock on the door, made the four women grow still. It was dark, and visitors did not normally come to their small home after dark. Margoth pushed her chair from the table and crept to the door. "Who's there?"

"An old friend."

"Wait, George?" Margoth unlocked the bolts on the door and pulled it open.

Before her stood the man who taught her how to put her talents to use. His micro loans delivered dozens of women out of poverty. That money was the reason Teresa's daughters were no longer offering themselves to truck drivers for food. It was the reason Ana had enough food to feed her child, she had been pregnant when they left the landfill. There was no way for her to know who the father had been, but her daughter had a future with the women that surrounded Ana with love and understanding. They looked out for her. That man was the reason Margoth had enough money to support the women in her home. One small loan and gentle guidance changed the lives of many families, not just the women. The children and the husbands ate better meals. The women were teaching their children a different way of life. These women could now afford to send their daughters to school, and when you give a girl the gift of education, the good deed never dies.

"Good evening, Margoth."

"Come in, it's been years." Margoth closed the door behind him and motioned for him to sit. "Do you want some food? I have more. I promise you will not be taking from us." She pointed to the dresser with a container full of beans and another with a cup of rice. There several tortillas and a papusa lay on a plate between the two containers.

"It looks like you're doing well. Is that the car you mentioned? And who are all these wonderful faces?" Ana's daughter climbed into Ana's lap.

"Oh, these are the women I told you about." Margoth introduced each to George. "This is Teresa, the mom and grandma, there is Ana with her daughter, Mara, and that is Paola."

George squinted in the dim lighting. As a general practice Margoth lit kerosene lamps and had one on the table. The other lamp they took to whatever corner they were in. The fireplace lit rest of the space. "It's nice to put a face to the stories." He took the seat offered.

Margoth handed him the papusa. "I'm so glad you made it back to Honduras."

"Me too," he bit the papusa. "What have you been up to?"

"I am working with Teresa, trying to get her business going. She uses recycled textiles to create new purses and clothes." Margoth grabbed a black suede bag from the pile on the floor. She was planning on putting it in her display at the restaurant.

"Isn't it lovely?"

George took the bag from Margoth and held it close to the lamplight. "The stitching is beautiful. Teresa, you made this from clothes in a landfill?"

The proud woman nodded. "I also make shoes, jackets, anything people wear."

"You have a talent for sure."

"George," Margoth said. "Do you think you could take a few and sell them at the mission house? We could put our story behind them. Let the customers know that when they buy an item with our label, they are helping a community."

George turned the bag over in his hand. "I can't see why not. I think that is a great idea. Do you have anymore? I can take them with me. After I talk to some of my colleagues, I'll get back to you. How much are you asking for a purse like this?"

Teresa fidgeted with her blouse. "I was asking five dollars. It takes a lot of work and five dollars for something that takes two days to make does not seem like a lot. If you think I should lower the cost, I will."

George leaned on his elbows on his knees. He took a moment before explaining. "Margoth, do you remember when I taught you how to look at your costs for opening your stand?" he asked.

"Yes, but I can't do that because the clothes are free," Margoth remembered.

"Then this is where we talked about opportunity costs. The tangible cost is one side. That is something you must pay, but the opportunity cost is the blood, sweat, and tears. These items that you are all making," he pointed at Teresa and the girls, "Have a huge amount of time invested. Don't change anything yet, but I think we could sell these back in the United States for at least twenty dollars."

Chapter 10
FINDING PEACE

Finding Peace

"George, I am teaching her independence and how to teach others, but she needs money. You can't make labels from scraps and buy thread with what she gets from the landfill. The dyes cost money, too. I'm being honest, your micro loan is the only reason I am in the position I am today. In ten years, I plan to buy the old orphanage and teach the young women how to farm. I want them to learn entrepreneurial skills. I see the strength and dedication in Teresa. She too wants to make a difference in other women's lives. She has taught the women in our community how to make these garments. I know she will be successful, and I am willing to help her make her loan payments if you can help her out. Please, think about it." Margoth presented her desire with no hidden agenda. She was a fierce, honest woman who worked hard. Her word was as good as gold. An old cliché that meant more in Honduras than most any other country.

George, put the purse in his lap and nibbled his papusa. "Before I give you an answer you know I have to go back and talk to the others. It is not all my decision. But I have the details to answer their questions, what exactly have you done Teresa? With your daughters, this house, the other women in the neighboring houses. Are you in the business women's bible study?"

Teresa's eyes glistened. Margoth had taken her to bible study with her in hopes that she would learn from the others. She made changes to her designs based on what she saw in discarded magazines at the landfill. Teresa was good at using her hands to separate fabrics but noticed that not all the women had the ability.

"Señor George, I promise you. I attend bible study every week with Margoth, and I go to church with Pastor David on Sunday. I teach the women how to sew, and how to separate seams, loosen and gather threads. We repurpose boots, blankets, and towels. We clean them on stones with water and soap. I have a special stone to brush the suede back to make it soft. My desire is to take what I do and invest the money in a building where I can store my supplies and have the women work along side of me." Teresa glanced at Margoth. "I want to have a place where the women can go to work and earn money improve their lives. They need money for medicine and school supplies for their children."

Margoth hugged her friend. "She has plans to help women who are afraid or don't want to start their own business. We know adding a loan payment is a lot of responsibility. But if the women work together, we believe the money will come. The co-op needs hands-on workers. We have a good community started here."

George looked at the papusa and finished it. When he was done chewing, he went to the Ana. "Are you willing to work with your mama? And can you commit to attending the business training we provide? The worst thing we could do for you is simply hand you a check and say "good luck."

Ana nodded and hugged Mara to her chest. Both mother and child stared at the man. "I want my daughter to learn that women can take are of each other. We can provide for our families. Together we are strong."

Paola hugged into her sister's side.

"You have done very well, Margoth. I believe Teresa has a good plan. I'll see you ladies, tomorrow evening. Buenos noches!"

George let himself out, Margoth secured the door behind him. She went back to her seat at the table and held Teresa's hand. The man had taken her finest purse yet.

"If he shows them that bag, Teresa, they won't deny us their assistance. We must get rest because tomorrow, while I am in the city, you need to gather the women and find out who is willing to be responsible for the money. The more women we get, the less each has to pay. This is the only the beginning. I believe in you, Teresa."

Mara ran to Teresa; the woman scooped her into her lap and kissed her head. "This is the first time I haven't had to worry about feeding our children. I go to sleep at night in a dry house with warmth and blankets. It is more than I could have hoped after my house was lost. I have more than I did even then. It's all thanks to you, Margoth. Even if it was the microloan George lent you to start your business. You have a mind for this. I never could have imagined people would want what I created from a landfill. Maybe I can't be happy, because I can't believe it is me who is taking the steps to make it happen. Are you happy Margoth?"

Margoth went to the dresser and scraped the beans into the rice. She stirred them, scraped them into a ceramic pot with a lid, and put it at the edge of the fireplace to keep it warm for morning. After lighting the candle in front of the Jesus statue in the corner she turned to Teresa.

"I don't know. What does it mean to be happy?" She sat back on her knees. "I guess I am." She turned to look at the women in the far corner, and then at Mara. "I am content. It is different. When I look at your daughters it makes me proud. They work together with the women here. Is that the same as happiness? I can't say. One time, I thought I was happy. Before my mama, died and my Juan went to the ministry. Now, I don't look at life as a day-to-day small piece of eternity. I want bigger and better. It's not enough living in the small house. We will make your business work because we need a home for us all," Margoth affirmed and pointed at the five of them.

The three girls and Teresa slept by the fireplace on alpaca blankets Margoth bought from the market. The vendor had alpaca thread and raw wool which she wanted Teresa to buy, if George came back with the micro-loan for Teresa's start-up materials. Margoth sat against the wall by the candle, watching the flame dance. It was tiny, but its flame lit the entire corner. When she looked back to the fireplace, she had an idea. What if she could get the orphanage with payments like she did the loan for George. She wouldn't have to wait, and she could take over the grounds. They could grow crops enough to feed more than the nine women and their families. They could grow crops to sell.

Just as important as the loan was the self-esteem that resulted in knowing the micro funds were not charity, but a legitimate business loan that would be paid back over time. These new entrepreneurs were empowered. Access to business capital had seen them on a course of financial independence , and breaking the cycle of poverty. Children are educated. Hope is achieved.

Margoth fell asleep dreaming about Alpacas, goats, chickens, and pigs running through the field behind the orphanage. They wouldn't have to buy many supplies if they used their own sources. "Am I happy?" she asked herself aloud. "I think I am."

#

Morning came and Teresa had removed the pot of beans and rice from the fireplace. She put the tortillas on a warm rock and went outside to gather water from the cistern. Ana had Mara feed the chickens as she followed along, teaching her the proper way to toss the vegetable scraps. Paola gathered whatever eggs they had and took them to the wash basin. All the women had chores and were grateful to have them. Even Mara was proud when a chicken ate the morsels she tossed to the ground.

Margoth smiled and called to Ana, "She is learning the joy in feeding a hungry creature."

"She might be one to work at your restaurant, instead of sewing. She likes to eat." Ana joked.

The three-year-old followed her mother to the house and took her place on the tattered blanket by the door. She knew that once the chores were done, it was time for breakfast. Today they had warm beans and rice in a tortilla with coffee. It was a good breakfast for an important day. Because whether George knew or not, Margoth felt that it was judgement day. Her mind raced with questions. *Did I show Teresa's intent to help the community? Should I have let her talk for herself? Would George trust me after all these years? Am I putting enough of myself out there for these women to succeed?*

"Breakfast!" Teresa called.

Mara and Ana sat on the floor, Paola stood by the dresser with Teresa, and Margoth sat at the table.

"May I say grace?" Paola asked.

"Of course," Margoth said.

"Lord our father, I ask you to look over Margoth as she goes to work in the city today. I ask you to help my mama get all the women to be a part of her project so señor George will say yes to the loan. And bless little Mara so she can grow up and never have to know what it is to go days without food and always have clothes. We thank you for this house, and the food we are about to receive. Amen."

The three women repeated, "Amen."

Mara had her eyes squeezed closed, "Amen."

The women ate in silence with the importance of the day keeping Margoth from focusing on her own needs. "I'm going to the orphanage after I drop off supplies to Carmen. I'll go to the restaurant after. Teresa goes to Ines, then the others. It is important to go to the eldest first. It shows respect, even if you believe they will say 'no', ask the women, and explain that they would be taking on a financial responsibility. But without money to back your business, you can't afford the supplies you need."

Margoth and Paola packed the car with boxes of banana leaves, bags of rice, and jars of spices. After the car was loaded Paola went back in the house while Margoth drove in the direction of her Nueva Suyapa shop.

#

Carmen stood outside the tamale shop. She had a wash rag wet with vinegar water, wiping the windows. "Margoth!"

"Hola, hermanita. How are you?" She went to the young woman. "Are you happy living with your man? If you had another place, would you leave?"

"You know I can't. He has ties to Carlos. I don't know what, and I won't ask. Please, Margoth. I've told you. I can run the shop, but that's all. He doesn't want me to go with you."

"And you're afraid you'll end up like mama," Margoth sighed.

"No, I'm afraid you will. They hurt you by taking what you love. You're all I've got. Don't push it, okay?" Carmen implored.

Margoth hugged her sister and whispered in her ear, "One day, you will be free, Carmen."

Her sister hugged her back, dripping water on the sidewalk. "Not if it hurts you."

Margoth unloaded the boxes from the car and helped Carmen put the spices away. She waited until Carmen's helper arrived before she left. She didn't ask, because she was ninety percent sure, Carmen's man had someone watching her sister. If not, then it was someone keeping watch on her sister to hurt her man. Either way, it wasn't good, and there were eyes on the shop that had no interest in helping women.

Margoth kissed her sister, and climbed in her car, scanning the street for familiar faces as she drove toward Tegucigalpa. Nothing stood out to her, but it didn't mean they weren't there.

#

The abandoned orphanage was a mile out of the way, down a dusty road. It was a large yellow building that had at one time been home to more than sixty children and their caregivers.

Although once prosperous and flush with government money, it fell onto hard times when the funding was diverted into the corrupt hands of bureaucrats. The place struggled to get by for a while, but when private donations slowed to a trickle, they were forced to shut their doors, leaving behind a single caretaker and a few workers who did their best to live off the land and keep the place up. It was more than they could handle. The asphalt shingles on the peaked roof were crumbling away and the door and window frames were warped from leaking water that rushed in during the monsoon season. Most of the children that had lived there were forced back onto the streets to beg and steal for enough to eat, or worse, coerced into abusive relationships.

A few scrawny chickens scurried into the weeds when Margoth pulled the car into the driveway. There was no real parking lot, only a patch of worn grass. Margoth turned off the car and sat for a few minutes looking at the building before she got out and walked up to the front door.

A rusty metal knocker was still attached to the turquoise door, paint peeling off in streaks revealing the worn wood beneath. Margoth lifted the metal ring and let it bounce off the plate. The sound reverberated through the building. "Hello?" she called. "Is anyone here?"

A few seconds later she heard the soft patter of bare feet before the door creaked open. A teenager's face appeared in the crack, looking out with large dark eyes. "May I help you?" she said.

MARGOTH | 113

"My name is Margoth, I have an appointment with señora Hernandez." Margoth smiled at the young woman. She noticed the girl's reservations. "I'll wait here while you get her."

"The girl closed the door and left Margoth to stand in the sun.

She walked back to her car and leaned on the hood taking in the condition of the property. There was an outbuilding made from concrete blocks, it's roof was flat and tin. A goat was tied to a tree by a tire swing. There was a power line attached to the edge of the roof suggesting that the building still had working electricity.

She let her mind wander as she imagined what could be done with this property. This place was more than an abandoned orphanage. It had vast potential and could be converted into a home and cooperative farm where women could work together.

"Margoth Cruz?"

Margoth snapped back into the moment. Christina?"

"We spoke on the phone. Let me show you around." Christina led Margoth on a tour of the property. It was old, and needed work, but it had everything necessary to build a new life for the women she was trying to help. A large building held several dorm-style apartments that she guessed could accommodate thirty or more people. The main building containing the dormitories also had a large open kitchen, and Margoth was astonished to see that the stoves and refrigerators appeared to be in working order. Christina said the large commercial oven had been donated by a church in Dallas. Several acres of productive-looking farmland were lush with corn, sorghum, and beans, though the weeds were starting to take over. Closing her eyes, Margoth could visualize several large greenhouses on the property, using drip-irrigation to grow peppers and tomatoes which could be sold to local stores and restaurants. She imagined women working diligently on the land while their children were taught in the large community room on the first level of the property. Margoth could almost smell the warm, yeasty aroma of fresh bread baking in the oven while laughing children ran through the house.

After the tour, Christina told Margoth that the building owner was anxious to sell. A young and somewhat affluent young man from Tegucigalpa, had inherited the property from his recently deceased father, and he wanted to take as much cash from the sale as he could and be done with it.

"Now that you have seen it, are you still interested in buying the place?"

"I am. Do you know the price?"

"He is asking only $15,000 for the property," said Christina

Margoth took a deep breath.

"My goal is to have a place where I can help establish a farming cooperative for several women and their families. I will have to find the funding someplace. This project is so important to the women I am working with. I am prepared to do what it takes. Even if it means I must wait a year."

The woman blinked at Margoth, "For what it is worth, I will put in a good word for you. I believe in what you are doing."

Margoth thanked Christina for the tour and walked back to her car, her head spinning. Could she do this? Was it even possible?

On the drive back home her head was filled with dreams of all that she could do with this property. She would make this work. She had to make this work.

Chapter 11
2011 SMALL GIFTS

118 | Jeffrey Hartman

2011 Small Gifts

Margoth peered out of the kitchen window over the sink. With the support of MercyLink, George, and the sweat equity of a dozen hard-working women community leaders, she found the backing necessary to acquire the orphanage. It wasn't an easy feat. They all agreed that they worked for the day that women would have value and for that to happen they needed to pave the way. Putting food on the table and children in school was the first step. Showing them that they can overcome the odds through collaboration.

"It takes a lot of hands to raise a village," Christina had said when she and Margoth met.

Margoth had Teresa make an embroidered piece for the wall with that exact saying. It hung from a single nail over the kitchen table. Having rooms and furniture was still new, but overdue. It did not matter that the table lost its luster, or that the fabric was worn. She and the women who resided with her knew they were blessed. The farm was a haven, and Margoth had George to thank for getting her own mission started.

A black car with tinted windows pulled onto the dirt drive. It raised the hackles on the back of her neck. A cold chill went down her spine. She wiped her hands on her apron and opened the door. She spotted Teresa hanging fresh washed clothes from a line she tied between the trees. The women folded her arms over her chest and looked toward Margoth. They both took several cautious steps toward the stranger.

The passenger side door opened, and Carmen climbed out with a duffel bag and suitcase. She had a red skirt and yellow T-shirt, spattered with fresh wet spots. Margoth stepped toward her little sister, studying her face. The black car sped off, leaving the three women in a cloud of dust. Carmen dropped her bags.

"Hermanita?" Margoth whispered. "What is happening?" Margoth stood before her and cupped her tear-streaked cheeks.

Carmen collapsed into her sister. "He let me go."

Margoth laughed and cried. "Carmen, I have missed you. But why, what made him change his mind?" She squeezed her sister. She scanned the driveway and tree line for unwanted eyes. "He does not like me, and now brings you here. Where I show women their strength and independence?" She could not keep the irony out of her voice. She cocked her brow and sought an answer for the alarming happenings.

Teresa also scanned the trees as she hurried across the worn grass drive. "Carmen, tell us." She clenched an old pillowcase dripping water on the dirt. The drops dried as fast as they fell. It was unbearably hot which raised the anxious tension that exuded from the women.

"Por favor, let me go inside. May I have some water?" Carmen asked. "She pushed back from her embrace with Margoth and used the corner of her shirt to blot her eyes.

"Of course," Margoth said. She took her sisters arm and led her to the door.

Teresa motioned to the women standing in the entrance door. They ran to the house; fear emanated from their faces. Carmen's businessman had ties to Carlos. The last thing any of them wanted was for Carlos to know they were there.

"Are we going to owe dues to Carlos if he finds out we are here? What if the other gangs come?" Ana asked.

Carmen stepped inside the door dragging her duffel bag. Margoth had the suitcase. "He won't tell Carlos because he wants to forget he ever knew me. I'm pregnant."

Margoth grabbed a cup and filled it with a pitcher of water from the counter. "Is that all you had to do?" the elder sister chided.

Tears streaked down Carmen's cheeks. "He has a wife with kids. I'm no good to him now." She used the dry corner of her shirt to dry her face again.

Paola handed her an embroidered handkerchief she made. While having pity for her daughter, she could not help feeling a rising sense of anger as she considered the prevailing religious beliefs that had caused so many unwelcome pregnancies in her community.

Carmen sat in a straight back chair at the large dining room table. "I don't know how many other women he has or had, but I think he kept me the longest. I was a girl when he claimed me. Now I am a woman with needs. I'm going to be a mama. That means a bed is not enough. I have to make food and keep a child." She sipped the water.

Margoth hugged her. The truth was that she didn't care why he let her sister go. She hated the man and wanted her sister back for years. She was twenty-six having her first child and Margoth was going to be there for her. All the women would be. "This is your home, now. I told you before and it remains true, my door is always open for you and now your child. I love you, Carmen."

There was another reality that Margoth realized the moment Carmen sat in the chair. Her sister was kept in a room for ten years. Her only outside contact was working in Margoth's tamale shop. Margoth would have to introduce her to the world she missed. It also meant that she would sell the shop in Nueva Suyapa. She didn't want to have a reason to remind any of the men that she or Carmen existed.

Teresa and the girls were at the farm as well as their old neighbor Ines and her daughter. Seven girls stayed after the sale of the orphanage. They were sixteen, seventeen, and eighteen at the time. Christina and Margoth decided the girls should have a choice in staying or relocating. All seven decided to stay. Even though their eighteenth birthdays came and went, they chose to stay when Margoth offered them room and board in exchange for their contribution to at least one of the co-ops. She accepted rent when they had something to put toward the loan payment.

The orphanage became a commune of sorts. Women from Nueva Suyapa that were part of the farming co-op came to tend the crops and livestock. Others who took part in Teresa's textile merchandising came to work in the outbuilding. It was a place where women networked. They learned how to craft and keep track of money. There was food, enough for them all to eat when they were there and to turn a profit. Not one woman or child would go hungry. Margoth left every morning for her restaurant in Tegucigalpa. On Sundays they all went to Pastor David's church, and nearly all of them attended Margoth's weekly bible study sessions. They had busy lives that gave them peace in the angst of gang violence and threats. But most of all, they had hope. The profits from the farm would make it possible for many of the children to go to their local high-school, and even have a good shot at attending the National University, transforming their lives forever.

#

Carmen had chosen to work with Margoth, but the older sister would present a new opportunity to the mother to be since she would soon have a baby to care for. Besides a busy city restaurant was a lot different from a small café in Nueva Suyapa.

"Hermanita," Margoth called.

"Mmmm?" Carmen had fallen asleep in a soft chair in the living room corner.

"You should consider taking part in the farm. There is no picking through landfills, only caring for the animals and land. I will lend you the money to put toward the co-op. You must buy in; make loan payments. If I pay them, you repay me. When you earn enough from the sales, you will be building a life and a future for your child."

"There is too much change, and I'm tired, Margoth. It seems like the world flew by while I dwelled in the shop and that room. I was alone, except when he wanted me. Now I am in a house filled with women and children. There is laughing, singing, and hard work. It is ridiculous, but I don't know how to feel. I want to go to the restaurant with you because I know food. When I have this baby, we can talk about the farm. But, right now, I want to be a part of Rosa's, the restaurant you named after Mama."

Margoth knelt by her sister. Tears glistened. "Another pair of seasoned hands is more than welcome in the kitchen. We will go tomorrow. Get some rest. It will be a long day." She kissed her sister's cheek and handed her a bunch of bananas. "Eat a banana, the babies grow strong when we have food."

Tegucigalpa was a large city. There were luxury hotels, malls, and larger parts where children begged for food. The odor from the Tegucigalpa landfill penetrated the air. On humid days there was no escape.

The square where Rosa called home was middle class. It was near the Art Gallery and nestled in a row of shops that sold purses, bags, and dresses. Teresa had a shop several doors down. She opened the store two years after she secured the micro loan from George. The co-op had grown to twenty-five women, all mothers who wanted to have enough to raise healthy children. A few of the women had decent, hard-working and loving husbands who served as good role models for the children, especially the young boys. And although men like these were the exception, rather than the rule in Honduras, they were nonetheless, a blessing indeed. Though one woman, Sara, defaulted on her payments several times because her husband refused to let her pay. She wasn't the first to have a dictating husband, and she wouldn't be the last. But just because she defaulted on a few months payments it didn't mean that she was out of the co-op. Instead, Teresa and the other women split her payment between them and covered the loan to George. They paid it off six months before Teresa signed the papers for the store front.

"Carmen will have to work in the kitchen until she learns the ways of a restaurant." Margoth said to Ines who was seated at the kitchen table sipping a cup of coffee. "She is tired and scared.

I know why she does not want to stay while I am gone. She is worried I will not return."

The women looked at Carmen asleep in the living room chair.

Ines sipped. "She was a slave to a man she didn't love and worked for years at a shop where her mother was murdered, under the threat of losing her only family. My farm co-op is here for when she has the child. But let her continue with what she knows. Her world is upside down, right now."

Margoth poured a cup of percolated coffee and took a tortilla with salt. She knew Ines was right. Her sister was better off doing what she knew and loved. As she bit her tortilla, she thought about how comforting it would be, not to tend the shop or worry about her sister. They would work together again.

She took her coffee to the living room and stood in the doorway. "Hermanita, you must be strong, and have courage. I am with you now. God has brought you home."

Chapter 12
2021 HOPE

128 | Jeffrey Hartman

2021 Hope

It was all Margoth hoped: to have those little children at her sister's sixteenth birthday party, live a life filled with food, love, and hope. Now she was a successful businesswoman, fighting feminine oppression and injustice, and serving as a role model for so many.

Ana was hard at work planting legumes, her slender figure bent in half, her hands skilled in the art of planting dancing their way along the tilled soil. Ines glanced at her from the kitchen window at the farm where she and eleven other women produced food to sell and feed their families. The number of women grew over the years and Margoth sent many of them to George to discuss business plans and how they could fulfill their dreams through MercyLink's Microfinance programs. At times a few dollars for documents, was all they needed. And all the women paid George's ministry back. They were determined women—devoted women.

Ines glanced back at her grandson in the woven bassinet she kept in the living room of the farmhouse. Margoth made the house large enough to bring orphans who were turned out on their eighteenth birthday. Most of which were women and needed a safe start. If there was one thing Pastor David and her friend George taught her, it was that education broke the poverty cycle. The young women worked on the farm in exchange for rent and learned how to start a business. Her sister Carmen joined her in her quest to help the women. She took them into Rosa's Restaurant to teach them how to use their crafts to better their lives. At the same time her daughter Rosa worked in the kitchen mixing masa dough or washing dishes. New and inexpensive texting apps allowed them to take food orders on cheap mobile phones, and some neighboring men helped them by delivering the food orders on their scooters. The community was alive and thriving. Healthy-looking children walked home from school in their smart uniforms, custom-made by the hands of a micro-loan funded woman.

Twenty years ago, Margoth was a woman with a dream. A dream that a passing stranger made possible. That man brought hope and courage to Honduras through his faith. The country was ravished by Hurricane Mitch's wrath. Orphans and homeless women made their way to the landfill in hope of finding money for food in the recyclables and shelter from discarded boxes. Through initiatives from missionary groups, the Honduran people have food, education, and awareness. Honduras itself is changing. The Tegucigalpa landfill has showers created with funds from the government for the people to have better sanitation.

Margoth continued to find women in need to show them how to change their status. Pastor David retired back to the United States after contracting COVID-19. Pastor Juan spoke before the congregation during an emotion-filled reunion at Pastor Dave's little church.

"Some of you may remember me," Pastor Juan said. His voice calm; fluid. "I lived here once. The small blue house at the bottom of the hill. It still stands, a new family dwells there now." He pointed to Margoth in the front pew. "I want to take this opportunity to thank the woman who showed me a path and encouraged me to follow it. That woman is Margoth. She took me in when I had no home. She fed me and gave me a job, a purpose. We all know God hears our pleas, but do we listen to his answers? Let me tell you then, of a single woman, a missionary, and a tamale stand…"

Margoth, Carmen, Teresa, Ines, Ana, Paola, and Mara all sat in the same pew. Carmen's daughter and Ines' grandson sat behind them. The women all joined hands, as Pastor Juan recounted the tale of Margoth and how a single act of kindness, grew to change an entire community.

#

After the service, Paola returned home. She was a middle-aged woman who worked the co-op when her children were at school. Her husband did not mind her working in the morning, so long as she was home in time to make dinner. He never questioned what she did during the day. He would eat and leave to meet his friends. It was a quiet life, and one that afforded her the ability to work for her family. Her children had clothes and shoes. They had a small wooden house with three rooms and beds. She worked tilling the soil that Ana now sowed. Their mother Teresa found she was not the only woman with a passion for the fabric arts. Her co-op became a model for other communities throughout Honduras. And her friend George took her black suede bag back to the United States with him. It hadn't taken long for orders to come in to fill shelves in American shops and department stores. Margoth helped create the tag giving credit to all the women who crafted the garments. It was a true collected labor for love.

Ines grew enough produce to sell to restaurants in Nueva Suyapa and Tegucigalpa. The crime in both cities was still rampant, but the government was changing hands. Local non-profit organizations with a focus on social justice were starting to make a difference, and it appeared for the first time in a very long time that the government was beginning to listen. Since experiencing the heartbreak of losing children to malnutrition, she made it her mission to feed the impoverished youth. She carried bins of vegetables that didn't sell to homeless families and children. She donated to the missions who put together food baskets that were delivered directly to the homes in Nueva Suyapa. The farm was now a home for women. A place where they could buy into an existing co-op or develop their own.

MercyLink was more active than ever, delivering capital to an increasing number of families that now numbered in the hundreds, and offering Margoth as a model for success.

As for Margoth, she has become a well-known advocate for change and continues to spread education to the women of Nueva Suyapa. She finds the seeds of education change each subsequent generation. You will often find her speaking in churches and community centers, touting the virtues of micro-business as a powerful force for good. She continues to fight for her neighbors as violent crimes against women are still rampant. In a world where a woman is murdered every sixteen hours, femicide goes without investigation, and street thugs collect their dues. But Margoth has an iron will, born from the strength of her faith; solidified by discord. "Have I not commanded you? Be strong and courageous. Do not be afraid; do not be discouraged, for the Lord your God will be with you wherever you go".

EPILOGUE

The one memory that has had perhaps the most significant impact on me since the beginning of my microfinance activities in desperate parts of the world occurred during a trip to Honduras in October of 2019. I was there to meet with a number of women that my non-profit organization, The CareLink Foundation, had selected for microfinance funding. It is always a joy to meet with these inspiring and courageous women, and to listen as they share their dreams for starting small businesses. I love it. We were having a successful trip, providing life-changing capital for several determined and grateful women who, freshly-empowered, would earn profits from their new businesses that would alter the trajectory of ether lives forever. **https://carelinkfoundation.org**

Taking a diversion from our microfinance activities, my team and I decided to help one of our partner organizations that was operating a free medical clinic out of a small church in Nueva Suyapa, a rough and dangerous little community near downtown Tegucigalpa. It was at this clinic that a life-altering memory was burned into my mind forever. It was near the end of the day. I was doing my best to hold a conversation with a charming and animated little Spanish-speaking girl of about ten years of age. She captivated my heart as I pondered what her future might hold. I silently thanked God that my own grandchildren, by virtue of winning the "Geography Lottery" would be spared such a likely dismal future.

At that moment, the little girl's pitiful-looking mother appeared and begged us to take her daughter back to the United States with us. It was a sobering and chilling experience. My heart broke as I considered that this sweet girl had no idea what misery she almost assuredly faced in the years to come. Perhaps even more distressing for me as a parent and grandparent, was the realization that the girls' mother would be a helpless witness to her child's suffering. I am often haunted by this memory, and the smiling but somehow sad face of that precious child, and the near-panic of her desperate mother. This memory has served to inspire me with a sense of urgency for the work we are doing.

Helping desperately poor people in the developing world is both the most challenging yet rewarding work I have ever done. It is difficult. It is often so frustrating. As an entrepreneur and former business owner I have always been pretty good at solving complex problems and getting things done. Even the simplest things in the developing world, however, can be quite difficult to accomplish. The delivery of goods you were waiting on never shows up because the driver was hijacked. The woman who launched her bakery is delayed three months as the commercial oven you purchased for her is held up at the factory because of power-outages. The money you are wiring to a bank in Honduras does not arrive in time because bureaucrats, acting in the interest of trying to identify suspicious drug-money transactions, have flagged your large cash transfer for review. The list goes on. In the midst of these frustrations, I have sometimes heard the enemy in my mind whisper to me that I should quit. After all, we are only able to help a relatively small segment of the 700 million desperately poor people in the world. What's the point? Why do this? Because nothing I have ever done, save raising my own children, has ever been so gratifying. I also believe that we are all called to *"Love your neighbor"*, (Mark 12:31), and the work I do is my humble attempt to do that.

IT'S ABOUT BELIEF

Providing microfinance loans is the primary focus of our non-profit, The CareLink Foundation. But we are really in the business of helping women believe in themselves. Nearly all of the people we serve are women, largely due to the fact that women in developing countries tend to suffer the most. They, and their children, are often marginalized and victimized by a legal and cultural bias that leaves them desperately poor, without opportunity, and literally helpless. We help them. When provided with working capital, women are more likely than men (at least in Third World Countries) to use those funds for investing in a business or to their family's benefit, than men. You have heard the expression, "when you give a man a fish, you feed him for a day, but when you teach a man to fish, you feed him for a lifetime." Well, I have heard it said that "If you teach a woman to fish, everyone eats!" I believe this is true.

Something supernatural happens when we help one of these women start a business. First of all, before lending them money (at zero percent interest, by the way), we provide them with formal business training and financial coaching. Armed with this information and funding, many of these women believe in themselves for the very first time. They believe they can achieve and succeed. They have self-confidence, renewed self-esteem, and hope. I am completely convinced that the "belief" we help instill in these inspiring women is just as important as the loans we provide.

The recipients of these loans also understand that it is the power of love that brought my organization to them. We always make sure these faith-filled women know that we are serving them in Jesus' name.

The chapters in this book paint a dark picture of Honduras; Extreme poverty, governmental corruption, social injustice, gang violence, and rampant crime are daily realities. And men, often consumed by alcoholism or drug addiction that frequently accompanies a feeling of hopelessness and desperation, regularly fall short of their duties as fathers and husbands. These factors, indeed, create a perfect storm of trouble and suffering for women and their children.

I recognize that men in general have not been portrayed in a particularly positive light in *"Because There Was Margoth."* A deeply-rooted "Machismo" social attitude is imbedded into the culture of Honduras and many other developing nations. This attitude is prevalent, and so many men have been raised to be oblivious to their responsibilities to treat women with honor and respect. As a result, many of the men mistreat women, shrug their fatherly responsibilities, and may even consider it a "badge of honor" to father a large number of children without considering how they will be cared for and financially supported. Other men, either seeking green pastures north of the border, or just running away, have simply abandoned their families. Still other men have been killed by gang violence, or have been so intimidated by gangs, and the lure of illegal gains, that they are of no use to their families. I have personally listened to many of the women we serve speak to me of this terrible reality with faces filled with tears. Women often find themselves alone in a harsh and dangerous land.

Regardless of the cause, men are often out of the picture, and so it is the courageous women that are left behind that we are all too often funding. I would be remiss, however, if I did not acknowledge the fact that there are, of course, many fine and God-fearing men in Honduras, and I have the privilege of working with many of them. I count them as friends, and they are rare and bright lights in the darkness.

WHY I WROTE THIS BOOK

I wrote this book for several reasons. My primary purpose is to hopefully inspire you to consider how you can use your own gifts and talents to make the world a better place. I do believe in God's Economy, we are all called to identify our skills and leverage them for good. And as for non-believers, most still believe in the principle of trying to leave the world just a little bit better, and that helping others is consistent with their admirable moral values. So, I will consider it a huge success if you find yourself motivated by Margoth, and seeking your own way to serve. Perhaps you will find your purpose in volunteering at a local food pantry. You may discover meaningful work in working with teams that build homes for disadvantaged persons. Others may believe that mentoring an at-risk student growing up in a broken home may be more aligned with their skills or passions. Or maybe, like me, you will sense a calling to serve in the challenging neighborhoods of the developing world. Still others, like my accountant friend Curt, may have a different view of service as he recently reminded me. "I can't do what you do, Jeff", my friend said, "but I can write checks!" And that, in a way, is service too.

Regardless of your calling, please seek it. I promise you will receive far more than you give. There is something very special that happens when you experience the joy of serving. You will receive a peace and sense of purpose that can not be found elsewhere. There is a confidence of well-being and alignment with the universe that occurs when a single person's passion for service intersects with the needs of humanity. This is true for any level of service, great or small.

The second reason I wrote this book was to draw attention to the unique power of microfinance in the developing world. My background is in business. I founded and ran a successful technology company for two decades and my family and I received the benefits of that business. While business, and Capitalism in general, have gotten a somewhat bad rap in recent years, there is no doubt in my mind that the economic benefits of business "lift all ships." Business can be a powerful force for good when kind and decent people use those profits for improving lives and creating opportunities for others. Microfinance empowers women. Armed with training, business skills, capital, and perhaps the community of a few other microfinance recipients, these new entrepreneurs can now do things that used to be impossible. They can afford to send their children to school and can provide more nutritious meals for their families. They can afford birth control and therefore determine when and how often they become pregnant. This reproductive empowerment may be the single most important variable in determining a woman's future economic status in the developing world. Microfinance women become independent and they can save for their future.

MICROFINANCE IS SUSTAINABLE

In addition to the empowering characteristic of microfinance capital, investing in local small businesses is also a sustainable way to help others. As micro loans are repaid, those funds are reinvested into other new businesses in the community, creating a cycle for good that generates growth, prosperity, and positive sustainable change.

Everyday, thousands of well-intended short-term mission teams fly into desperately poor regions of the globe to provide food, medicine, medical clinics, and clothing. Many of these groups are sponsored by North American churches and the participants speak fondly of their experience of gratification and achieving a renewed spirituality through their service. Unfortunately, the impact of those groups is limited. Those good people will get back on airplanes and fly home in a week and the mother they served at the medical clinic will once again be trying to comfort her child suffering from chronic diarrhea next month when the free medicine runs out. This is not a sustainable approach.

Let me be very clear, these short-term mission trips are a good and necessary thing. Reducing human suffering, even for a brief time, is good. But this type of service is just not sustainable unless it addresses the root cause of suffering. I also want to acknowledge that these short-term mission trips do play an important role in introducing North Americans, particularly young people, to the value, necessity, and God-requested nature of service. And there is, of course, immeasurable good in showing our remote "neighbors" that there are good people in the world trying to live-out the "love your neighbor" mandate. A poor and suffering person may find new hope from an ambassador of Christ who shows-up with much-needed free medicine. I have no argument with this loving service. And it should and must continue. I have participated in many of these with my wife Kathy and my children (now grown), Jennifer and Jeff, on may occasions. I do believe, however, that the most impactful and long-lasting solutions to world suffering must be sustainable. Microfinance is sustainable.

And finally, Microfinance is effective because it "pays forward." For example, a woman operating a small but profitable micro-business can afford to send her children to school, making them far less likely to fall prey to gangs, poverty, or unwanted pregnancies. A girl who graduates from high school will have a chance at attending college. She has a dramatically improved employment outlook. She is far less-likely to live a life of chronic poverty. She has hope. She has a future. And so one small loan can have a dramatic and positive impact for generations to come.

WHY HELP THE DEVELOPING WORLD?

I am often asked why my organization helps people in Third World countries, and not the United States. It is a valid question asked by sincere and thoughtful people. Good people. Although it is true that my organization is currently only operating in the developing world, we are examining the possibility of expanding in the U.S. In the meantime, our services are directed to some of the poorest people on Earth. The reasons for our focus on the developing world are simple; suffering in the Third World is typically more severe than in developed areas. A "poor" person in the United States, for example, often has access to food stamps, food pantries, subsidized medical insurance, and other social safety nets. They probably have a smart phone, a computer, a television, and a car. Such things are unthinkable luxuries in the developing world, where extremely poor people live on a dollar per day.

HOPE

Because there was Margoth takes place in Honduras, a beautiful country populated by many wonderful people. Honduras is a very troubled place, however. As is always the case, the factors contributing to the sad state of affairs on Honduras, like many other developing countries, is complicated. Some of the problems are the result of simple bad luck, or the meddling of other countries. A large measure of the problems facing Honduras, however, are self-inflicted harm exacerbated by governmental corruption, greed, and immoral human behavior. The result is a dysfunctional infrastructure, wide-spread crime, gangs, poverty, social injustice, lack of opportunity, and a feeling of hopelessness.

Despite these truths, there is reason for hope. Just a few short years ago Honduras was literally the murder capital of the world, and gangs and police corruption were out of control. The kidnapping of North Americans visiting Honduras by drug cartels for the purpose of raising money through ransom was a constant and real threat. On more than one occasion, my team and I were forced to leave a neighborhood when gangs presented themselves, and we were in danger. A dear friend of mine was robbed by a gang member while we stood outside a church in Nueva Suyapa. Things were really bad. They are better now, and improving.

Newly-elected governmental officials, sometimes motivated by social justice organizations, have taken big strides toward stemming corruption. At the time of this writing, a new president, who ran on an anti-corruption platform, has been recently elected. Thousands of corrupt police officers, for example, have been terminated or convicted of crimes. The on-going reformation of a corrupt and broken school system has resulted in a dramatic increase in the numbers of days that students are in class, an important contributing metric when measuring an effective education system. Beyond that, the current Honduran justice system has extradited dozens of suspected drug dealers in the past few years, including the notorious brother of a former Honduran president. At the time of this writing, a Honduran judge has approved the extradition of a former Honduran president to the United States to face drug trafficking charges. Legislation has been enacted, and court cases won, that have restored an important measure of justice for employees, poor rural land-owners, and women's rights initiatives.

So, there is still much work to do in continuing to create an infrastructure that will sustain real change and prosperity, but things are moving in the right direction.

MOVING FORWARD

The ultimate end-game for any non-profit seeking to improve conditions for disadvantaged persons is to put themselves out of work, and the developing world, when measured with most economic metrics, is gradually improving. Extreme world poverty, for example, tracked by the World Bank, has been nearly halved in the last decade. But considering that over 700 million people in the world are still living in extreme poverty, we can see that organizations like mine have much work to do, and there is no risk of putting ourselves out of business in the near future.

As you seek your own way to utilize your gifts and talents, please know that the "where" you serve is far less important than the "how". As you work to identify your purpose, through brainstorming, consulting with friends, or prayer, you may find yourself volunteering at a local homeless shelter, or helping your church do yard work for elderly members of the community. Or, you may end-up teaching financial planning to a group of women in Haiti. Perhaps you are already actively serving in a meaningful way. Congratulations! Perhaps you are simply interested in a new way to serve, or in expanding your reach and impact. The readers guide at the end of this book, and some of the discussion questions will, I hope, help you chart your course.

Regardless of your "where," my wish for you is that you will find your purpose and experience the fulfillment that I know is awaiting you. And remember, you will not be alone in your journey. *"Have I not commanded you? Be strong and courageous, do not be afraid; do not be discouraged, for the Lord your God will be with you wherever you go."*

A READERS' GUIDE

Chapter 1: Post Hurricane Mitch

1. Have you ever seen "The Butterfly Effect" in action?
   – Describe.

2. Have you ever been to a Third World Country?
   – What was that like?
   – Were you ever afraid during your visit?
   – Were you shocked by the dramatic contrast between prosperity and poverty?

3. Some people when visiting a luxury resort in an extremely poor country, for example, are unsettled by neighboring areas that are so poor and destitute.
   – Have you experienced this?
   – Did this trouble you?

Chapter 2: Feliz Cumpleaños

1. Many in Honduras are a part of the 700 million people in the world living in extreme poverty. The World Bank defines extreme poverty as living on $1.90 per day or less.
   - Was there ever a time in your life when you considered yourself "poor"?
   - Can you remember how much you were earning at that time?
2. Despite their poverty, Margoth and her family and friends find joy in a simple birthday celebration with barely enough food to share.
   - Do you think the families celebrating a typical North American birthday are any more joyful?
3. Margoth's favorite "go to verse" is Joshua 1:9.
   - Read that text.
   - Why would that verse be so important to Margoth?
   - Do you have a verse (or perhaps a quote or "saying") that you meditate on when seeking comfort, strength or courage?

Chapter 3: New Friends

1. Some people encounter an extremely traumatic experience - like a devastating hurricane - and become stronger. Others just barely survive and cope.
   – What explains the difference in these people?

2. Have you ever performed any disaster relief work?
   – Describe

3. Why did you decide to perform this relief assistance?

4. Describe how you felt when you experienced this service.
   – Did this experience change you?
   – How?

Chapter 4: Inspiration

1. Violence is a constant fear for many Honduran women.
    - Do you know anyone who has had to deal with violence in their life?
    - How did experiencing a violent situation impact them?

2. Some Hondurans try to flee the difficulty of their country in search of a better life in the Unites States.
    - How do we balance our desire, and perhaps moral obligation, to show compassion for these people with the need for national security?

3. Margoth is presented with an opportunity to launch a micro-business, but there are risks.
    - What are the risks?
    - What would you do?
    - Have you ever taken a similar risk?

4. Many women receiving Microfinance funding and training are inspired to believe in themselves for the first time.
    - Why is "belief" such a powerful force?

Chapter 5: 2002 Opening Day

1. Have you ever been in any situation in which you experienced real fear?
   – Describe

2. George claims that "Love your neighbor" (Matthew 12:31) and "Faith without action is dead" (James 2:17) are two principles that motivate him to serve others.
   – Do you believe "action" is required in order to be a person of "faith"?

3. So much of what Margoth does is done with others in mind. For example, she is careful to document her work to create a record that might be useful for other women.
   – Do you know anyone in your community who is like this?

Chapter 6: Spring

1. Margoth seems almost obsessed with helping others and being a role model.
   – Do you know anyone like Margoth?
2. Has anyone like Margoth had an influence on you?
3. The faith of many Honduran women is very important to them.
   – Why?
   – Do you think faith has a more significant role in the daily life of the average Honduran compared to the average North American?
   – Why?

Chapter 7: Injustice

1. For many people in developing countries, violent death is a daily reality. Margoth uses the emotion of the death of her mother to inspire her to provide a good life, and a huge opportunity, for Juan. In this case, an event meant for "bad" was transformed into something "good."
   – Have you ever experienced a life event that seemed "bad," but over time it worked out for "good"?

2. Have you ever felt the emotion of an observed social injustice that affected you in such a powerful manner you wanted to take action?
   – Did you act?
   – Why or why not?

Chapter 8: Perseverance

1. Has the death of a loved one ever inspired you to want to live a better life?
2. Can you think of the life (or death) of a famous person that has inspired you to become your best self?
   – Describe.
3. Death reminds us that our days are numbered. There is a saying that reminds us that we each have only a certain number of "High Quality Days Remaining," ("HQDRs").
   – Do you believe you are doing your best to make the best of your HQDRs?

Chapter 9: Overcoming

1. Margoth's investment in Teresa (one of Margoth's microfinance protégées) impacted the lives of Teresa and her daughters forever.
   - Has there been anyone in your life that had faith in you and made an "investment" in your future that changed your life in a big way?

2. Margoth's interest in Teresa's life, and the resulting profits from a microfinance loan have created an opportunity for Teresa's daughters to go to school, a rare gift that changes lives for generations to come.
   - What role did education play in your own life
   - How would your life be different without the education you received, or the contacts and friends you made at school?

3. Microfinance is often described as "Empowering."
   - What does empowerment mean?

Chapter 10: Finding Peace

1. The emotion of losing her mother and the burden of responsibility of looking after others has taken somewhat of a toll on Margoth. She contemplates whether or not she is truly happy.
   - Have you ever felt the stress or anxiety related to a burden to help others, when the needs seem too great for you to endure?

2. Margoth seems to push her own emotions aside, and accelerate her drive do work harder to help other women as a way ignoring her own feelings of unhappiness. Helping others can be stressful.
   ¬ Can you relate to this in any way?

Chapter 11: Small Gifts

1. Carmen becomes the victim of a common casualty in Honduras; a pregnancy followed by abandonment by her unborn child's father. Margoth considers it a "gift" that Carmen has returned to her, and is now safe.
   - Do you know anyone that experienced an unwanted pregnancy but then put her own interests aside to have and raise the child?
   - What was their economic situation?

2. The "Machismo" culture in Honduras encourages some men to father as many children as possible, even if they can not, or will not, financially support them. Lack of access to contraceptives, a strict religious culture, and a violent and alcoholic husband can make it almost impossible for some women to control how many children they have.
   - What would you do if you were in this situation?

3. Microfinance initiatives are often most successful when small groups of women work together in a community for the common good of their business "cooperative."
   - Why do you think this approach is more likely to succeed than funding women individually?

Chapter 12: Hope

1. Juan's life was forever changed when he walked from the Tegucigalpa landfill and into Margoth's life. He is now a Pastor and because of Margoth's act of loving kindness toward him, he is well-positioned to help many others. Although his prospects as a little boy were grim, indeed, he is a now a success.
    - Looking back at your life, can you remember a time when an opportunity presented to you drastically altered the trajectory of your future for the better?

2. Hope and faith play a huge role in the lives of many people living in hardship. We have all experienced difficulties in life, but probably not as extreme as Margoth and her friends and family.
    - How has hope helped you handle adversity?
    - How would you describe hope?
    - Do you have hope despite so many difficulties in the world today?
    - What is the reason for your hope?

Challenge Questions

1. Before reading this book, were you familiar with the concept of microfinance lending?
   - Did Margoth's story change your view of microfinance?
2. Some people believe that it is better to donate to charitable causes "closer to home" rather than helping international relief efforts.
   - What is your viewpoint?
3. How does the principle of "Love your Neighbor" play into question #2 above?
   - Has cable television, the internet, and immediate news coverage of international human suffering enlarged your view of who your neighbors are?
4. Jeff believes "Investor," rather than "donor" is a more appropriate term to describe someone who financially contributes to microfinance causes.
   - Can you see the difference?
   - Describe.
5. Consider the differences between the types of "Charity"; giving poor people things; free food, for example, (a "hand out"), versus the sustainability of helping them start a business, (a "hand-up").
   - In which category do you place most of your charitable "Investments"?
   - Why is sustainability so critical to making meaningful positive change?

6. Has this book changed your perception of severely disadvantaged people in developing countries?
   – How?

7. Do you think the characteristics of courage, grit, and perseverance personified in Margoth are more prevalent in women facing challenges as compared to men?

8. Do you believe in the concept of "We are our brother's keeper?"
   – Why or why not?

9. Before reading this book, did you know that approximately 700 million people in the world are living in extreme poverty?
   – Has this fact had an impression on you?
   – How?

10. Margoth's faith is a major source of her drive and courage.
    – Can you relate to this?

11. Do you believe people like George and Margoth are part of a divine providential plan, or simply random persons doing good deeds?
    – Explain.

12. Have you ever considered going on an international mission trip?
    – Why or why not?

13. Toward the end of the book, the wide-reaching ramifications of "one good deed" are illuminated.
    – Consider how this "Butterfly Effect" can impact the world.
14. Did this book cause you to consider your own level of giving or service for the greater good?
    – How?
15. Do you believe we have a moral or spiritual imperative to serve others?
    – Consider what this means.
16. Individuals represented in this book derive deep joy from serving others.
    – Can you think of a time when you experienced this?
17. How would you describe your satisfaction with your current level of service or giving?
    – Are you willing to take intentional action to change this?
    – How?

Seven Steps to Finding Your Purpose

"Where your talents and the world's need cross, there lies your calling." - Aristotle

In the last several years we have seen an increase in charitable giving and service in the United States. For Christians, acts of service are considered the natural result of our faith. Doing "good works" is the joyful reaction to an attitude of gratitude. Most people have a desire to "give back", but may not know how to get started, especially with so many good causes to choose from. I believe a person's first priority for giving and service should be their own church. If you are satisfying your gifting goals to your church, and are feeling called to go above and beyond, these seven steps can help you get started.

1. **Acknowledge God's invitation to serve.** Many people believe we are "called" to serve. Do you believe this?
2. **Consider your gifts.** Service is most gratifying when your skills are well-aligned with your perceived calling and you feel well-equipped.
3. **Pray about this.** Seek God's wisdom.
4. **Get advice and counsel** from trusted friends and family.
5. **Consider your comfort zone.** Would you consider international service work? Perhaps local needs are more in-line with your risk-tolerance.

6. **Research options**. Your own church leadership will likely have good insight into the local needs of your community, and even international mission opportunities, that require volunteers or funding. It starts with your church. Ask friends and colleagues about charities they may be involved with. Leverage your network. You can also visit **jeffreyhartman.org** for a list of well-regarded causes in our resources section. Of course, the internet is rich with opportunities, but discernment is important. Do your homework.

7. **Volunteer and assess**. Select a charity and volunteer. (Perhaps with a friend?). Move on if you are not satisfied. If you are able, give with your time and your treasure. There are many worthy causes with missions aligned with your world-view and interests.

ABOUT THE AUTHOR

Jeffrey Hartman is an innovative entrepreneur and author with a passion for helping individuals improve their lives through the power of Microfinance. The president of The CareLink Foundation, a faith-based non-profit that distributes Microfinance capital to individuals in the developing world, Jeff has helped people launch small businesses in desperately poor regions of the globe for over a decade. Jeff is also the founder of Thirsty Child, an organization committed to eliminating the suffering of children who lack access to clean, safe drinking water in the Third World.

He and his wife, Katherine, have two grown children and four grandchildren, and live in Naperville, Illinois and New Buffalo, Michigan.

https://JeffreyHartman.org

CPSIA information can be obtained
at www.ICGtesting.com
Printed in the USA
JSHW061425180722
28231JS00005B/18

9 798885 810043